Promises of Comfort

from

GOD'S WORD

BakerBooks

a division of Baker Publishing Group
Grand Rapids, Michigan

Contents

When You Can't Stop . . .

When You Need . . .

Introduction

When disaster strikes or we're hurting in some way, we want tangible comfort. A sympathetic hug. A comforting word. A warm shoulder to cry on. This is the language of comfort in which we're fluent. In the agony of our souls, we turn to that which provides what we need.

The Creator of the universe—the Shepherd of our souls—also seeks to console. Yet the comfort He offers goes beyond our limited notions of true comfort. As God declares, "My thoughts are not your thoughts, and my ways are not your ways. . . . Just as the heavens are higher than the earth, so my ways are higher than your ways, and my thoughts are higher than your thoughts" (Isaiah 55:8-9).

There is comfort to be had in the deep places of His Word—comfort that comes in surprising forms. God promises deep and abiding rest for our souls (Matthew 11:28-30). Within the pages of this book, you'll find hundreds of words of comfort. You'll also find a small, comforting message, like a Post-It from God on your soul. May you find rest for your soul.

When You're . . .

Abandoned/Neglected

The LORD your God is a merciful God. He will not abandon you, destroy you, or forget the promise to your ancestors that he swore he would keep.

Deuteronomy 4:31

Be strong and courageous. Don't tremble! Don't be afraid of them! The LORD your God is the one who is going with you. He won't abandon you or leave you.

Deuteronomy 31:6

The Lord is the one who is going ahead of you. He will be with you. He won't abandon you or leave you. So don't be afraid or terrified.

Deuteronomy 31:8

May the Lord our God be with us as he was with our ancestors. May he never leave us or abandon us.

1 Kings 8:57

Even if my father and mother abandon me,
   the LORD will take care of me.

Psalm 27:10

The LORD is good.
   He is a fortress in the day of trouble.
   He knows those who seek shelter in him.

Nahum 1:7

God has said, "I will never abandon you or leave you." So we can confidently say,

> "The Lord is my helper.
> I will not be afraid.
> What can mortals do to me?"

> Hebrews 13:5-6

He said to me, "It has happened! I am the A and the Z, the beginning and the end. I will give a drink from the fountain filled with the water of life to anyone who is thirsty. It won't cost anything. Everyone who wins the victory will inherit these things. I will be their God, and they will be my children."

> Revelation 21:6-7

Abused/Used by Others

"Because oppressed people are robbed
  and needy people groan,
I will now arise," says the LORD.
"I will provide safety for those who long for it."

Psalm 12:5

Guard me as if I were the pupil in your eye.
Hide me in the shadow of your wings.

Psalm 17:8

He reached down from high above
  and took hold of me.
He pulled me out of the raging water.
He rescued me from my strong enemy
  and from those who hated me,
    because they were too strong for me.

Psalm 18:16-17

On the day when I faced disaster, they confronted me,
  but the LORD came to my defense.
    He brought me out to a wide-open place.
    He rescued me because he was pleased with me.

Psalm 18:18-19

Do not be so far away, O LORD.
Come quickly to help me, O my strength.

Rescue my soul from the sword,
   my life from vicious dogs.
Save me from the mouth of the lion
   and from the horns of wild oxen.

Psalm 22:19-21

My eyes are always on the LORD.
   He removes my feet from traps.

Psalm 25:15

He hides me in his shelter when there is trouble.
He keeps me hidden in his tent.
He sets me high on a rock.

Psalm 27:5

The LORD confronts those who do evil
   in order to wipe out all memory of them
      from the earth.
Righteous people cry out.
   The LORD hears and rescues them
      from all their troubles.

Psalm 34:16-17

All my bones will say, "O LORD, who can compare
   with you?
   You rescue the weak person from the one
      who is too strong for him
      and weak and needy people from the one
         who robs them."

Psalm 35:10

Do not be preoccupied with evildoers.
Do not envy those who do wicked things.

They will quickly dry up like grass
  and wither away like green plants.
                    Psalm 37:1-2

God is my helper!
The Lord is the provider for my life.
                    Psalm 54:4

You have been my refuge,
  a tower of strength against the enemy.
I would like to be a guest in your tent forever
  and to take refuge under the protection
    of your wings. *Selah*
                    Psalm 61:3-4

As I lie on my bed, I remember you.
  Through the long hours of the night,
    I think about you.
You have been my help.
  In the shadow of your wings, I sing joyfully.
My soul clings to you.
  Your right hand supports me.
                    Psalm 63:6-8

Hear my voice, O God, when I complain.
Protect my life from a terrifying enemy.
Hide me from the secret plots of criminals,
  from the mob of troublemakers.
    They sharpen their tongues like swords.
    They aim bitter words like arrows
      to shoot at innocent people
        from their hiding places.

They shoot at them suddenly,
>   without any fear.

>>   Psalm 64:1-4

The God who is in his holy dwelling place
>   is the father of the fatherless
>>   and the defender of widows.

>>   Psalm 68:5

Oppressed people will see this and rejoice.
May the hearts of those who look to God for help
>   be refreshed.

The LORD listens to needy people.
He does not despise his own who are in prison.
Let heaven and earth, the seas,
>   and everything that moves in them, praise him.

>>   Psalm 69:32-34

He is the one who will rescue you from hunters' traps
>   and from deadly plagues.
He will cover you with his feathers,
>   and under his wings you will find refuge.
>>   His truth is your shield and armor.

>>   Psalm 91:3-4

Because you love me, I will rescue you.
>   I will protect you because you know my name.
When you call to me, I will answer you.
>   I will be with you when you are in trouble.
>   I will save you and honor you.
>   I will satisfy you with a long life.
>   I will show you how I will save you.

>>   Psalm 91:14-16

The LORD is merciful and righteous.
Our God is compassionate.
The LORD protects defenseless people.
   When I was weak, he saved me.
Be at peace again, my soul,
   because the LORD has been good to you.

Psalm 116:5-7

I know that the LORD will defend the rights
      of those who are oppressed
   and the cause of those who are needy.
      Indeed, righteous people will give thanks
         to your name.
      Decent people will live in your presence.

Psalm 140:12-13

Pay attention to my cry for help
   because I am very weak.
Rescue me from those who pursue me
   because they are too strong for me.
Release my soul from prison
   so that I may give thanks to your name.
      Righteous people will surround me
         because you are good to me.

Psalm 142:6-7

The LORD protects foreigners.
The LORD gives relief to orphans and widows.
   But he keeps wicked people
      from reaching their goal.

Psalm 146:9

It is good to sing psalms to our God.
It is pleasant to sing his praise beautifully.

The Lord is the builder of Jerusalem.
    He is the one who gathers the outcasts
        of Israel together.
    He is the healer of the brokenhearted.
    He is the one who bandages their wounds.

                              Psalm 147:1-3

The Lord tears down the house
        of an arrogant person,
    but he protects the property of widows.

                              Proverbs 15:25

Do not rob the poor because they are poor
    or trample on the rights of an oppressed person
        at the city gate,
    because the Lord will plead their case
        and will take the lives of those who rob them.

                              Proverbs 22:22-23

Every word of God has proven to be true.
    He is a shield to those who come to him
        for protection.

                              Proverbs 30:5

    Your husband is your maker.
        His name is the Lord of Armies.
    Your defender is the Holy One of Israel.
        He is called the God of the whole earth.

                              Isaiah 54:5

The Lord is faithful and will strengthen you and protect
you against the evil one.

                              2 Thessalonians 3:3

Afraid

He renews my soul.
He guides me along the paths of righteousness
    for the sake of his name.
Even though I walk through the dark valley
  of death,
    because you are with me, I fear no harm.
      Your rod and your staff give me courage.

                         Psalm 23:3-4

The LORD is my light and my salvation.
  Who is there to fear?
The LORD is my life's fortress.
  Who is there to be afraid of?

                      Psalm 27:1

God is our refuge and strength,
  an ever-present help in times of trouble.
That is why we are not afraid
  even when the earth quakes
    or the mountains topple
      into the depths of the sea.
    Water roars and foams,
      and mountains shake at the surging waves.

                    Psalm 46:1-3

I trust God.
I am not afraid.
   What can mortals do to me?
                Psalm 56:11

You do not need to fear
  terrors of the night,
  arrows that fly during the day,
  plagues that roam the dark,
  epidemics that strike at noon.
     They will not come near you,
       even though a thousand may fall dead
          beside you
       or ten thousand at your right side.

You only have to look with your eyes
  to see the punishment of wicked people.
                Psalm 91:5-8

Strengthen limp hands.
Steady weak knees.
Tell those who are terrified,
  "Be brave; don't be afraid.
    Your God will come with vengeance, with divine
      revenge.
    He will come and rescue you."
                Isaiah 35:3-4

Don't be afraid, because I am with you.
Don't be intimidated; I am your God.
  I will strengthen you.
  I will help you.
  I will support you with my victorious right hand.
                Isaiah 41:10

I alone am the one who comforts you.
Why, then, are you afraid of mortals, who must die,
of humans, who are like grass?

Isaiah 51:12

Aren't five sparrows sold for two cents? God doesn't forget any of them. Even every hair on your head has been counted. Don't be afraid! You are worth more than many sparrows.

Luke 12:6-7

People who do what is right don't have to be afraid of the government. But people who do what is wrong should be afraid of it. Would you like to live without being afraid of the government? Do what is right, and it will praise you.

Romans 13:3

God didn't give us a cowardly spirit but a spirit of power, love, and good judgment.

2 Timothy 1:7

No fear exists where his love is. Rather, perfect love gets rid of fear, because fear involves punishment. The person who lives in fear doesn't have perfect love.

1 John 4:18

When I saw him, I fell down at his feet like a dead man. Then he laid his right hand on me and said, "Don't be afraid! I am the first and the last, the living one. I was dead, but now I am alive forever. I have the keys of death and hell."

Revelation 1:17-18

Aging

The LORD has kept me alive as he promised. It's been 45 years since Israel wandered in the desert when the LORD made this promise to Moses. So now look at me today. I'm 85 years old. I'm still as fit to go to war now as I was when Moses sent me out.

Joshua 14:10-11

O God, you have taught me ever since I was young,
and I still talk about the miracles you have done.
Even when I am old and gray, do not abandon me,
O God.
Let me live to tell the people of this age
what your strength has accomplished,
to tell about your power to all who will come.

Psalm 71:17-18

O Lord, you have been our refuge
throughout every generation.
Before the mountains were born,
before you gave birth to the earth and the world,
you were God.
You are God from everlasting to everlasting.

Psalm 90:1-2

Righteous people flourish like palm trees
and grow tall like the cedars in Lebanon.
They are planted in the LORD's house.

They blossom in our God's courtyards.
　　Even when they are old, they still bear fruit.
　　They are always healthy and fresh.
　　　　They make it known that the LORD is decent.
　　　　He is my rock.
　　　　He is never unfair.

Psalm 92:12-15

Silver hair is a beautiful crown found
　　in a righteous life.

Proverbs 16:31

Grandchildren are the crown of grandparents,
　　and parents are the glory of their children.

Proverbs 17:6

　　Even when you're old, I'll take care of you.
　　Even when your hair turns gray, I'll
　　　　support you.
I made you and will continue to care for you.
I'll support you and save you.

Isaiah 46:4

Angry

Let go of anger, and leave rage behind.
  Do not be preoccupied.
    It only leads to evil.

Psalm 37:8

But he is compassionate.
  He forgave their sin.
    He did not destroy them.
  He restrained his anger many times.
    He did not display all of his fury.

Psalm 78:38

A gentle answer turns away rage,
  but a harsh word stirs up anger.
The tongues of wise people give good expression
    to knowledge,
  but the mouths of fools pour out a flood
    of stupidity.
The eyes of the LORD are everywhere.
  They watch evil people and good people.
A soothing tongue is a tree of life,
  but a deceitful tongue breaks the spirit.

Proverbs 15:1, 4

A gift given in secret calms anger,
  and a secret bribe calms great fury.

Proverbs 21:14

Mockers create an uproar in a city,
but wise people turn away anger.

Proverbs 29:8

Don't be quick to get angry, because anger is typical of fools.

Ecclesiastes 7:9

Be angry without sinning. Don't go to bed angry.

Ephesians 4:26

Get rid of your anger, hot tempers, hatred, cursing, obscene language, and all similar sins.

Colossians 3:8

Anxious/Stressed

Let go of your concerns!
　　Then you will know that I am God.
　　　I rule the nations.
　　　I rule the earth.

Psalm 46:10

When I worried about many things,
　　your assuring words soothed my soul.

Psalm 94:19

But first, be concerned about his kingdom and what has his approval. Then all these things will be provided for you. So don't ever worry about tomorrow. After all, tomorrow will worry about itself. Each day has enough trouble of its own.

Matthew 6:33-34

As they were traveling along, Jesus went into a village. A woman named Martha welcomed him into her home. She had a sister named Mary. Mary sat at the Lord's feet and listened to him talk.

But Martha was upset about all the work she had to do. So she asked, "Lord, don't you care that my sister has left me to do the work all by myself? Tell her to help me."

The Lord answered her, "Martha, Martha! You worry and fuss about a lot of things. There's only one thing you need. Mary has made the right choice, and that one thing will not be taken away from her."

Luke 10:38-42

Don't be troubled. Believe in God, and believe in me. My Father's house has many rooms. If that were not true, would I have told you that I'm going to prepare a place for you? If I go to prepare a place for you, I will come again. Then I will bring you into my presence so that you will be where I am.

John 14:1-3

Never worry about anything. But in every situation let God know what you need in prayers and requests while giving thanks. Then God's peace, which goes beyond anything we can imagine, will guard your thoughts and emotions through Christ Jesus.

Philippians 4:6-7

Turn all your anxiety over to God because he cares for you.

1 Peter 5:7

Ashamed

To you, O LORD, I lift my soul.
I trust you, O my God.
    Do not let me be put to shame.
    Do not let my enemies triumph over me.
No one who waits for you will ever be put to shame,
    but all who are unfaithful will be put to shame.

                                Psalm 25:1-3

I pray that my ways may become firmly established
    so that I can obey your laws.
        Then I will never feel ashamed
            when I study all your commandments.

                              Psalm 119:5-6

The Almighty LORD helps me.
    That is why I will not be ashamed.
        I have set my face like a flint.
            I know that I will not be put to shame.

                              Isaiah 50:7

He was wounded for our rebellious acts.
He was crushed for our sins.
    He was punished so that we could have peace,
    and we received healing from his wounds.

                              Isaiah 53:5

Don't be afraid, because you won't be put to shame.
Don't be discouraged, because you won't be disgraced.
    You'll forget the shame you've had since you were
        young.
    You won't remember the disgrace of your husband's
        death anymore.

Isaiah 54:4

You will have plenty to eat, and you will be full.
    You will praise the name of the Lord your God,
        who has performed miracles for you.
        My people will never be ashamed again.

Joel 2:26

At that time
    I will deal with all who have overpowered you.
    I will rescue those who are lame.
    I will gather those who have been scattered.
    I will make them praised and famous in all the world,
        though they had been ashamed.

Zephaniah 3:19

Scripture says, "Whoever believes in him will not be ashamed."

Romans 10:11

Never be ashamed to tell others about our Lord or be ashamed of me, his prisoner. Instead, by God's power, join me in suffering for the sake of the Good News.

2 Timothy 1:8

If you suffer, you shouldn't suffer for being a murderer, thief, criminal, or troublemaker. If you suffer for being a Christian, don't feel ashamed, but praise God for being called that name.

1 Peter 4:15-16

Backsliding

The fear of the LORD is pure.
   It endures forever.
The decisions of the LORD are true.
   They are completely fair.
   They are more desirable than gold,
      even the finest gold.
   They are sweeter than honey,
        even the drippings from a honeycomb.
    As your servant I am warned by them.
      There is a great reward in following them.

Psalm 19:9-11

But you, Lord our God, are compassionate and forgiving, although we have rebelled against you.

Daniel 9:9

You were doing so well. Who stopped you from being influenced by the truth? The arguments of the person who is influencing you do not come from the one who is calling you. A little yeast spreads through the whole batch of dough. The Lord gives me confidence that you will not disagree with this. However, the one who is confusing you will suffer God's judgment regardless of who he is.

Galatians 5:7-10

God saved you through faith as an act of kindness. You had nothing to do with it. Being saved is a gift from God. It's not the result of anything you've done, so no one can brag about it. God has made us what we are. He has created us in Christ Jesus to live lives filled with good works that he has prepared for us to do.

Ephesians 2:8-10

If a person thinks that he is religious but can't control his tongue, he is fooling himself. That person's religion is worthless. Pure, unstained religion, according to God our Father, is to take care of orphans and widows when they suffer and to remain uncorrupted by this world.

James 1:26-27

You have endured, suffered trouble because of my name, and have not grown weary. However, I have this against you: The love you had at first is gone. Remember how far you have fallen. Return to me and change the way you think and act, and do what you did at first.

Revelation 2:3-4

Barely Coping

You make a wide path for me to walk on
  so that my feet do not slip.

> 2 Samuel 22:37

He has kept us alive
  and has not allowed us to fall.

> Psalm 66:9

When I said, "My feet are slipping,"
  your mercy, O Lord, continued to hold me up.

> Psalm 94:18

The Lord supports everyone who falls.
He straightens the backs of those who are bent over.
  The eyes of all creatures look to you,
    and you give them their food at the proper time.

> Psalm 145:14-15

The Lord Almighty is my strength.
  He makes my feet like those of a deer.
    He makes me walk on the mountains.

> Habakkuk 3:19

God can guard you so that you don't fall and so that you can be full of joy as you stand in his glorious presence without fault. Before time began, now, and for eternity glory, majesty, power, and authority belong to the only God, our Savior, through Jesus Christ our Lord. Amen.

> Jude 24-25

Bitter

Don't take revenge, dear friends. Instead, let God's anger take care of it. After all, Scripture says, "I alone have the right to take revenge. I will pay back, says the Lord."

Romans 12:19

Get rid of your bitterness, hot tempers, anger, loud quarreling, cursing, and hatred.

Ephesians 4:31

Fathers, don't make your children bitter about life. Instead, bring them up in Christian discipline and instruction.

Ephesians 6:4

Do everything without complaining or arguing.

Philippians 2:14

Never imitate evil, but imitate good. The person who does good is from God. The person who does evil has never seen God.

3 John 11

Childless

The LORD said, "I promise I'll come back to you next year at this time, and your wife Sarah will have a son."

Sarah happened to be listening at the entrance of the tent, which was behind him. Abraham and Sarah were old. Sarah was past the age of childbearing. And so Sarah laughed to herself, thinking, "Now that I've become old, will I enjoy myself again? What's more, my husband is old!"

The LORD asked Abraham, "Why did Sarah laugh and say, 'Can I really have a child now that I'm old?' Is anything too hard for the LORD? I will come back to you next year at this time, and Sarah will have a son."

Because she was afraid, Sarah denied that she had laughed. But the LORD said, "Yes, you did laugh."

Genesis 18:9-15

Early in the morning Elkanah and his family got up and worshiped in front of the LORD. Then they returned home to Ramah. Elkanah made love to his wife Hannah, and the LORD remembered her. Hannah became pregnant and gave birth to a son. She named him Samuel [God Hears], because she said, "I asked the LORD for him."

1 Samuel 1:19-20

Be strong, all who wait with hope for the LORD,
    and let your heart be courageous.

Psalm 31:24

Turn your burdens over to the LORD,
    and he will take care of you.
        He will never let the righteous person stumble.

Psalm 55:22

Sing with joy, you childless women
    who never gave birth to children.
Break into shouts of joy,
    you women who never had birth pains.
    "There will be more children
        of women who have been deserted
        than there are children of married women," says
            the LORD.
Expand the space of your tent.
    Stretch out the curtains of your tent, and don't hold
        back.
        Lengthen your tent ropes, and drive in the tent
            pegs.
You will spread out to the right and left.
    Your descendants will take over other nations,
        and they will resettle deserted cities.
Don't be afraid, because you won't be put to shame.
Don't be discouraged, because you won't be disgraced.
    You'll forget the shame you've had since you were
        young.

Isaiah 54:1-4

I am forced to deal with a recurring problem. . . . I begged
the Lord three times to take it away from me. But he told
me: "My kindness is all you need. My power is strongest

when you are weak." So I will brag even more about my weaknesses in order that Christ's power will live in me. Therefore, I accept weakness, mistreatment, hardship, persecution, and difficulties suffered for Christ. It's clear that when I'm weak, I'm strong.

2 Corinthians 12:7-10

Confused

Yet, I am always with you.
    You hold on to my right hand.
        With your advice you guide me,
            and in the end you will take me to glory.

                                    Psalm 73:23-24

The LORD will continually guide you
    and satisfy you even in sun-baked places.
He will strengthen your bones.
    You will become like a watered garden
        and like a spring whose water does not stop
            flowing.

                                    Isaiah 58:11

Brothers and sisters, in view of all we have just shared about God's compassion, I encourage you to offer your bodies as living sacrifices, dedicated to God and pleasing to him. This kind of worship is appropriate for you. Don't become like the people of this world. Instead, change the way you think. Then you will always be able to determine what God really wants—what is good, pleasing, and perfect.

                                  Romans 12:1-2

We have the mind of Christ.
    1 Corinthians 2:16

God is not a God of disorder but a God of peace.

1 Corinthians 14:33

The weapons we use in our fight are not made by humans. Rather, they are powerful weapons from God. With them we destroy people's defenses, that is, their arguments and all their intellectual arrogance that oppose the knowledge of God. We take every thought captive so that it is obedient to Christ.

2 Corinthians 10:4-5

Considering an Abortion

The fear of the LORD is the beginning of wisdom.
Good sense is shown by everyone
    who follows God's guiding principles.
His praise continues forever.

Psalm 111:10

You alone created my inner being.
You knitted me together inside my mother.

Psalm 139:13

My bones were not hidden from you
    when I was being made in secret,
    when I was being skillfully woven
        in an underground workshop.
Your eyes saw me when I was only a fetus.
    Every day of my life was recorded in your book
        before one of them had taken place.

Psalm 139:15-16

Before I formed you in the womb,
    I knew you.
Before you were born,
    I set you apart for my holy purpose.
    I appointed you to be a prophet to the nations.

Jeremiah 1:5

Criticized/Condemned

Open criticism is better than unexpressed love.

Proverbs 27:5

Wounds made by a friend are intended to help,
but an enemy's kisses are too much to bear.

Proverbs 27:6

God loved the world this way: He gave his only Son so
that everyone who believes in him will not die but will
have eternal life. God sent his Son into the world, not to
condemn the world, but to save the world.

John 3:16-17

Those who believe in him won't be condemned. But those
who don't believe are already condemned because they
don't believe in God's only Son.

John 3:18

So those who are believers in Christ Jesus can no longer
be condemned. The standards of the Spirit, who gives life
through Christ Jesus, have set you free from the standards
of sin and death.

Romans 8:1-2

Who will accuse those whom God has chosen? God has
approved of them. Who will condemn them? Christ has

died, and more importantly, he was brought back to life. Christ has the highest position in heaven. Christ also intercedes for us.

Romans 8:33-34

This is how we will know that we belong to the truth and how we will be reassured in his presence. Whenever our conscience condemns us, we will be reassured that God is greater than our conscience and knows everything. Dear friends, if our conscience doesn't condemn us, we can boldly look to God and receive from him anything we ask. We receive it because we obey his commandments and do what pleases him.

1 John 3:19-21

Depressed/Discouraged

My soul is discouraged.
    That is why I will remember you
        in the land of Jordan, on the peaks of Hermon,
            on Mount Mizar.
    One deep sea calls to another at the roar
        of your waterspouts.
    All the whitecaps on your waves have swept over me.
The LORD commands his mercy during the day,
    and at night his song is with me—
        a prayer to the God of my life.

Psalm 42:6-8

Remember the word you gave me.
    Through it you gave me hope.
This is my comfort in my misery:
    Your promise gave me a new life.

Psalm 119:49-50

You will be established in righteousness.
You will be far from oppression,
    so you will not be afraid.
You will be far from destruction,
    so it won't come near you.

Isaiah 54:14

Praise the God and Father of our Lord Jesus Christ! He is the Father who is compassionate and the God who gives comfort. He comforts us whenever we suffer. That is why whenever other people suffer, we are able to comfort them by using the same comfort we have received from God.

2 Corinthians 1:3-4

Yet God, who comforts those who are dejected, comforted us.

2 Corinthians 7:6

Finally, brothers and sisters, keep your thoughts on whatever is right or deserves praise: things that are true, honorable, fair, pure, acceptable, or commendable.

Philippians 4:8

Disabled

I will give thanks to you
  because I have been so amazingly
    and miraculously made.
      Your works are miraculous,
        and my soul is fully aware of this.

Psalm 139:14

Jesus was teaching in a synagogue on the day of worship. A woman who was possessed by a spirit was there. The spirit had disabled her for 18 years. She was hunched over and couldn't stand up straight. When Jesus saw her, he called her to come to him and said, "Woman, you are free from your disability." He placed his hands on her, and she immediately stood up straight and praised God.

Luke 13:10-13

As Jesus walked along, he saw a man who had been born blind. His disciples asked him, "Rabbi, why was this man born blind? Did he or his parents sin?" Jesus answered, "Neither this man nor his parents sinned. Instead, he was born blind so that God could show what he can do for him."

John 9:1-3

We know that all things work together for the good of those who love God—those whom he has called according to his plan.

Romans 8:28

Disillusioned/Apathetic

"My thoughts are not your thoughts,
   and my ways are not your ways," declares the LORD.
"Just as the heavens are higher than the earth,
   so my ways are higher than your ways,
      and my thoughts are higher than your thoughts."

Isaiah 55:8-9

Therefore, everyone who hears what I say and obeys it will be like a wise person who built a house on rock. Rain poured, and floods came. Winds blew and beat against that house. But it did not collapse, because its foundation was on rock. Everyone who hears what I say but doesn't obey it will be like a foolish person who built a house on sand. Rain poured, and floods came. Winds blew and struck that house. It collapsed, and the result was a total disaster.

Matthew 7:24-27

When John was in prison, he heard about the things Christ had done. So he sent his disciples to ask Jesus, "Are you the one who is coming, or should we look for someone else?" Jesus answered John's disciples, "Go back, and tell John what you hear and see: Blind people see again, lame people are walking, those with skin diseases are made clean, deaf people hear again, dead people are brought back to life, and poor people hear the Good News. Whoever doesn't lose his faith in me is indeed blessed."

Matthew 11:2-6

Do your best to present yourself to God as a tried-and-true worker who isn't ashamed to teach the word of truth correctly. Avoid pointless discussions. People who pay attention to these pointless discussions will become more ungodly, and what they say will spread like cancer.

2 Timothy 2:15-17

God's promise that we may enter his place of rest still stands. We are afraid that some of you think you won't enter his place of rest. We have heard the same Good News that your ancestors heard. But the message didn't help those who heard it in the past because they didn't believe. . . . So we must make every effort to enter that place of rest. Then no one will be lost by following the example of those who refused to obey.

Hebrews 4:1-2, 11

Divorced

"The LORD has called you as if you were
  a wife who was abandoned and in grief,
  a wife who married young and was rejected," says
    your God.
                                          Isaiah 54:6

I know the plans that I have for you, declares the LORD.
They are plans for peace and not disaster, plans to give you
a future filled with hope.
                                          Jeremiah 29:11

The Pharisees asked him, "Why, then, did Moses order a
man to give his wife a written notice to divorce her?"
  Jesus answered them, "Moses allowed you to divorce
your wives because you're heartless. It was never this way
in the beginning."
                                          Matthew 19:7-8

God our Father loved us and by his kindness gave us everlasting encouragement and good hope. Together with our
Lord Jesus Christ, may he encourage and strengthen you
to do and say everything that is good.
                                          2 Thessalonians 2:16-17

If any of you needs wisdom to know what you should
do, you should ask God, and he will give it to you. God is
generous to everyone and doesn't find fault with them.
                                          James 1:5

Feeling Hopeless

His anger lasts only a moment.
His favor lasts a lifetime.
  Weeping may last for the night,
    but there is a song of joy in the morning.

                                            Psalm 30:5

Help me God, as you promised, so that I may live.
  Do not turn my hope into disappointment.
Hold me, and I will be safe,
  and I will always respect your laws.

                                      Psalm 119:116-117

There is lasting peace for those who love your
    teachings.
  Nothing can make those people stumble.
I have waited with hope for you to save me, O LORD.
I have carried out your commandments.

                                      Psalm 119:165-166

Delayed hope makes one sick at heart,
  but a fulfilled longing is a tree of life.

                                        Proverbs 13:12

I will make rivers flow on bare hilltops.
I will make springs flow through valleys.
  I will turn deserts into lakes.
  I will turn dry land into springs.

I will plant cedar, acacia, myrtle, and wild olive
  trees in the desert.
I will place cedar, fir, and cypress trees together in
  the wilderness.
People will see and know.
Together they will consider and understand
  that the LORD's power has done this,
  that the Holy One of Israel has created it.

Isaiah 41:18-20

This is what the LORD says:

Forget what happened in the past,
  and do not dwell on events from long ago.
I am going to do something new.
  It is already happening. Don't you recognize it?
  I will clear a way in the desert.
  I will make rivers on dry land.

Isaiah 43:17-19

The reason I can still find hope
  is that I keep this one thing in mind:
the LORD's mercy.
  We were not completely wiped out.
  His compassion is never limited.
    It is new every morning.
    His faithfulness is great.

Lamentations 3:21-23

The sign of the Son of Man will appear in the sky. All the
people on earth will cry in agony when they see the Son of
Man coming on the clouds in the sky with power and great
glory. He will send out his angels with a loud trumpet call,
and from every direction under the sky, they will gather
those whom God has chosen.

Matthew 24:30

A thief comes to steal, kill, and destroy. But I came so that my sheep will have life and so that they will have everything they need.

John 10:10

[Jesus said,] You heard me tell you, "I'm going away, but I'm coming back to you." If you loved me, you would be glad that I'm going to the Father, because the Father is greater than I am. I'm telling you this now before it happens. When it does happen, you will believe. The ruler of this world has no power over me.

John 14:28-30

May God, the source of hope, fill you with joy and peace through your faith in him. Then you will overflow with hope by the power of the Holy Spirit.

Romans 15:13

There is one body and one Spirit. In the same way you were called to share one hope. There is one Lord, one faith, one baptism, one God and Father of all, who is over everything, through everything, and in everything.

Ephesians 4:4-6

We are telling you what the Lord taught. We who are still alive when the Lord comes will not go into his kingdom ahead of those who have already died. The Lord will come from heaven with a command, with the voice of the archangel, and with the trumpet call of God. First, the dead who believed in Christ will come back to life. Then, together with them, we who are still alive will be taken in the clouds to meet the Lord in the air. In this way we will always be with the Lord. So then, comfort each other with these words!

1 Thessalonians 4:15-18

Feeling like a Failure

The LORD is my inheritance and my cup.
  You are the one who determines my destiny.
  Your boundary lines mark out
    pleasant places for me.
Indeed, my inheritance is something beautiful.

  Psalm 16:5-6

The LORD is near to those whose hearts are humble.
He saves those whose spirits are crushed.

  Psalm 34:18

  Why are you discouraged, my soul?
  Why are you so restless?
    Put your hope in God,
      because I will still praise him.
        He is my savior and my God.

  Psalm 42:11

I look up toward the mountains.
  Where can I find help?
My help comes from the LORD,
  the maker of heaven and earth.
He will not let you fall.
  Your guardian will not fall asleep.
Indeed, the Guardian of Israel never rests or sleeps.

  Psalm 121:1-4

The Lord is your guardian.
The Lord is the shade over your right hand.
  The sun will not beat down on you during the day,
    nor will the moon at night.
The Lord guards you from every evil.
  He guards your life.
The Lord guards you as you come and go,
  now and forever.

Psalm 121:5-8

The Almighty Lord is coming with power
  to rule with authority.
His reward is with him,
  and the people he has won arrive ahead of him.
Like a shepherd he takes care of his flock.
  He gathers the lambs in his arms.
  He carries them in his arms.
  He gently helps the sheep and their lambs.

Isaiah 40:10-11

You will be established in righteousness.
You will be far from oppression,
  so you will not be afraid.
You will be far from destruction,
  so it won't come near you.

Isaiah 54:14

Why is my pain unending
  and my wound incurable, refusing to heal?
Will you disappoint me like a stream
  that dries up in summertime?

This is what the Lord says:

  If you will return, I will take you back.

Jeremiah 15:18-19

I'm convinced that God, who began this good work in you, will carry it through to completion on the day of Christ Jesus.

Philippians 1:6

The God of peace brought the great shepherd of the sheep, our Lord Jesus, back to life through the blood of an eternal promise. May this God of peace prepare you to do every good thing he wants. May he work in us through Jesus Christ to do what is pleasing to him. Glory belongs to Jesus Christ forever. Amen.

Hebrews 13:20-21

Ill

Blessed is the one who has concern for helpless people.
  The LORD will rescue him in times of trouble.
  The LORD will protect him and keep him alive.
    He will be blessed in the land.
      Do not place him at the mercy of his enemies.
  The LORD will support him on his sickbed.
    You will restore this person to health when he is ill.

I said, "O LORD, have pity on me!
  Heal my soul because I have sinned against you."

Psalm 41:1-4

When Jesus went to Peter's house, he saw Peter's mother-in-law in bed with a fever. Jesus touched her hand, and the fever went away. So she got up and prepared a meal for him.

Matthew 8:14-15

In the evening the people brought him many who were possessed by demons. He forced the evil spirits out of people with a command and cured everyone who was sick. So what the prophet Isaiah had said came true: "He took away our weaknesses and removed our diseases."

Matthew 8:16-17

Just then a woman who had suffered for twelve years with constant bleeding came up behind him. She touched the fringe of his robe, for she thought, "If I can just touch his robe, I will be healed." Jesus turned around, and when he saw her he said, "Daughter, be encouraged! Your faith has made you well." And the woman was healed at that moment.

Matthew 9:20-22

Then Jesus said, "Come to me, all of you who are weary and carry heavy burdens, and I will give you rest. Take my yoke upon you. Let me teach you, because I am humble and gentle at heart, and you will find rest for your souls. For my yoke is easy to bear, and the burden I give you is light."

Matthew 11:28-30

Then a man with a serious skin disease came to him. The man fell to his knees and begged Jesus, "If you're willing, you can make me clean." Jesus felt sorry for him, reached out, touched him, and said, "I'm willing. So be clean!" Immediately, his skin disease went away, and he was clean.

Mark 1:40-42

If any of you are having trouble, pray. If you are happy, sing psalms. If you are sick, call for the church leaders. Have them pray for you and anoint you with olive oil in the name of the Lord. (Prayers offered in faith will save those who are sick, and the Lord will cure them.) If you have sinned, you will be forgiven.

James 5:13-15

Impoverished

Jabez was more honorable than his brothers. His mother had named him Jabez [Painful], because she said that his birth was painful. Jabez prayed to the God of Israel, "Please bless me and give me more territory. May your power be with me and free me from evil so that I will not be in pain." God gave him what he prayed for.

1 Chronicles 4:9-10

You prepare a banquet for me
   while my enemies watch.
You anoint my head with oil.
   My cup overflows.

Certainly, goodness and mercy will stay close to me
   all the days of my life,
and I will remain in the LORD's house
   for days without end.

Psalm 23:5-6

The LORD knows the daily struggles
   of innocent people.
   Their inheritance will last forever.
They will not be put to shame in trying times.
Even in times of famine they will be satisfied.

Psalm 37:18-19

Every creature in the forest,
    even the cattle on a thousand hills, is mine.

Psalm 50:10

You satisfy my soul with the richest foods.
    My mouth will sing your praise with joyful lips.

Psalm 63:5

    But now he lifts needy people high
        above suffering
    and makes their families like flocks.
        Decent people will see this and rejoice,
        but all the wicked people
            will shut their mouths.

Let those who think they are wise
    pay attention to these things
        so that they may understand the LORD's blessings.

Psalm 107:41-43

Who is like the LORD our God?
    He is seated on his high throne.
    He bends down to look at heaven and earth.
    He lifts the poor from the dust.
    He lifts the needy from a garbage heap.
    He seats them with influential people,
        with the influential leaders of his people.
    He makes a woman who is in a childless home
        a joyful mother.

Psalm 113:5-9

You make water gush from springs into valleys.
    It flows between the mountains.
        Every wild animal drinks from them.
        Wild donkeys quench their thirst.

The birds live by the streams.
They sing among the branches.
You water the mountains from your home above.
You fill the earth with the fruits of your labors.

You make grass grow for cattle
and make vegetables for humans to use
in order to get food from the ground.

Psalm 104:10-14

What a large number of things you have made,
O Lord!
You made them all by wisdom.
The earth is filled with your creatures.
The sea is so big and wide
with countless creatures,
living things both large and small.
Ships sail on it,
and Leviathan, which you made, plays in it.
All of them look to you to give them their food
at the right time.
You give it to them, and they gather it up.
You open your hand,
and they are filled with blessings.

Psalm 104:24-28

Our help is in the name of the Lord,
the maker of heaven and earth.

Psalm 124:8

Blessed are all who fear the Lord
and live his way.

You will certainly eat what your own hands
   have provided.
   Blessings to you!
   May things go well for you!

Psalm 128:1-2

You open your hand,
   and you satisfy the desire of every living thing.
The LORD is fair in all his ways
   and faithful in everything he does.

Psalm 145:16-17

When that day comes, the LORD will give you relief
   from your pain and suffering,
   from the hard slavery you were forced to do.

Isaiah 14:3

The poor and needy are looking for water, but there
   is none.
   Their tongues are parched with thirst.
I, the LORD, will answer them.
I, the God of Israel, will not abandon them.

Isaiah 41:17

Ask the LORD for rain in the springtime.
   The LORD makes thunderstorms.
   He gives everyone rain showers for the plants in the
   field.

Zechariah 10:1

If your child asks you for bread, would any of you give
him a stone? Or if your child asks for a fish, would you
give him a snake? Even though you're evil, you know how

to give good gifts to your children. So how much more will your Father in heaven give good things to those who ask him?

Matthew 7:9-11

When they came to Capernaum, the collectors of the temple tax came to Peter. They asked him, "Doesn't your teacher pay the temple tax?"

"Certainly," he answered.

Peter went into the house. Before he could speak, Jesus asked him, "What do you think, Simon? From whom do the kings of the world collect fees or taxes? Is it from their family members or from other people?"

"From other people," Peter answered.

Jesus said to him, "Then the family members are exempt. However, so that we don't create a scandal, go to the sea and throw in a hook. Take the first fish that you catch. Open its mouth, and you will find a coin. Give that coin to them for you and me."

Matthew 17:24-27

Jesus said to them, "I can guarantee this truth: Moses didn't give you bread from heaven, but my Father gives you the true bread from heaven. God's bread is the man who comes from heaven and gives life to the world." They said to him, "Sir, give us this bread all the time." Jesus told them, "I am the bread of life. Whoever comes to me will never become hungry, and whoever believes in me will never become thirsty."

John 6:32-35

If you ask the Father for anything in my name, he will give it to you. So far you haven't asked for anything in my name. Ask and you will receive so that you can be completely happy.

John 16:23-24

Praise the God and Father of our Lord Jesus Christ! Through Christ, God has blessed us with every spiritual blessing that heaven has to offer.

Ephesians 1:3

My God will richly fill your every need in a glorious way through Christ Jesus.

Philippians 4:19

A godly life brings huge profits to people who are content with what they have. We didn't bring anything into the world, and we can't take anything out of it. As long as we have food and clothes, we should be satisfied.

1 Timothy 6:6-8

Insulted

All who see me make fun of me.
    Insults pour from their mouths.
        They shake their heads and say,
            "Put yourself in the LORD's hands.
                Let the LORD save him!
                Let God rescue him
                    since he is pleased with him!"

The LORD has not despised or been disgusted
    with the plight of the oppressed one.
        He has not hidden his face from that person.
           The LORD heard when that oppressed person
        cried out to him for help.

                          Psalm 22:7-8, 24

Give thanks to the LORD because he is good,
                because his mercy endures forever.

He remembered us when we were humiliated—
                    because his mercy endures forever.
He snatched us from the grasp of our enemies—
                    because his mercy endures forever.
He gives food to every living creature—
                    because his mercy endures forever.

Give thanks to the God of heaven
                    because his mercy endures forever.
                                Psalm 136:1, 23-26

Even though I walk into the middle of trouble,
    you guard my life against the anger of my enemies.
    You stretch out your hand,
        and your right hand saves me.
The LORD will do everything for me.
O LORD, your mercy endures forever.
Do not let go of what your hands have made.
                                Psalm 138:7-8

Lonely

The LORD answered, "My presence will go with you, and
I will give you peace."

Exodus 33:14

You make the path of life known to me.
    Complete joy is in your presence.
        Pleasures are by your side forever.

Psalm 16:11

The Messenger of the LORD camps around those
        who fear him,
    and he rescues them.
Taste and see that the LORD is good.
    Blessed is the person who takes refuge in him.

Psalm 34:7-8

The LORD of Armies is with us.
The God of Jacob is our stronghold. *Selah*

Psalm 46:7, 11

This God is our God forever and ever.
    He will lead us beyond death.

Psalm 48:14

As long as I have you,
    I don't need anyone else in heaven or on earth.

My body and mind may waste away,
  but God remains the foundation of my life
  and my inheritance forever.

Psalm 73:25-26

Being united with God is my highest good.
  I have made the Almighty LORD my refuge
  so that I may report everything that he has done.

Psalm 73:28

Whoever lives under the shelter of the Most High
  will remain in the shadow of the Almighty.
I will say to the LORD,
  "You are my refuge and my fortress,
  my God in whom I trust."

Psalm 91:1-2

Where can I go to get away from your Spirit?
Where can I run to get away from you?
  If I go up to heaven, you are there.
  If I make my bed in hell, you are there.
  If I climb upward on the rays of the morning sun
  or land on the most distant shore of the sea
  where the sun sets,
  even there your hand would guide me
  and your right hand would hold on to me.

Psalm 139:7-10

The LORD your God is with you.
  He is a hero who saves you.
  He happily rejoices over you,
  renews you with his love,
  and celebrates over you with shouts of joy.

Zephaniah 3:17

Remember that I am always with you until the end of time.

Matthew 28:20

I will ask the Father, and he will give you another helper who will be with you forever. That helper is the Spirit of Truth. The world cannot accept him, because it doesn't see or know him. You know him, because he lives with you and will be in you.

John 14:16-17

I will not leave you all alone. I will come back to you. In a little while the world will no longer see me, but you will see me. You will live because I live. On that day you will know that I am in my Father and that you are in me and that I am in you.

John 14:18-20

The one who is in you is greater than the one who is in the world.

1 John 4:4

Overwhelmed

Joseph said to them, "Don't be afraid! I can't take God's place. Even though you planned evil against me, God planned good to come out of it. This was to keep many people alive, as he is doing now."

Genesis 50:19-20

The LORD should be praised.
I called on him, and I was saved from my enemies.

The ropes of death had become tangled around me.
The torrents of destruction had overwhelmed me.
The ropes of the grave had surrounded me.
The clutches of death had confronted me.

I called on the LORD in my distress.
I cried to my God for help.
He heard my voice from his temple,
and my cry for help reached his ears.

Psalm 18:3-6

You have done many miraculous things,
O LORD my God.
You have made many wonderful plans for us.
No one compares to you!
I will tell others about your miracles,
which are more than I can count.

Psalm 40:5

God has promised the following
    through his holiness:
    "I will triumph!"

Give us help against the enemy
    because human assistance is worthless.
        With God we will display great strength.
        He will trample our enemies.

Psalm 108:7, 12-13

It is better to depend on the L<small>ORD</small>
    than to trust mortals.
It is better to depend on the L<small>ORD</small>
    than to trust influential people.

Psalm 118:8-9

A voice cries out in the desert:

"Clear a way for the L<small>ORD</small>.
Make a straight highway in the wilderness for
    our God.
    Every valley will be raised.
    Every mountain and hill will be lowered.
    Steep places will be made level.
    Rough places will be made smooth.
Then the L<small>ORD</small>'s glory will be revealed
    and all people will see it together.
        The L<small>ORD</small> has spoken."

Isaiah 40:3-5

Don't you know?
    Haven't you heard?
The eternal God, the L<small>ORD</small>, the Creator of the ends of
    the earth,
    doesn't grow tired or become weary.

His understanding is beyond reach.
He gives strength to those who grow tired
    and increases the strength of those who are weak.
Even young people grow tired and become weary,
    and young men will stumble and fall.

                                Isaiah 40:28-30

I will deal with all who have overpowered you.
I will rescue those who are lame.
I will gather those who have been scattered.
I will make them praised and famous in all the
    world,
    though they had been ashamed.

                                Zephaniah 3:19

Blessed are those who recognize they are spiritually
    helpless.
    The kingdom of heaven belongs to them.

                                Matthew 5:3

When Jesus came near, he spoke to them. He said, "All
authority in heaven and on earth has been given to me."

                                Matthew 28:18

But nothing is impossible for God.

                            Luke 1:37

Panicking

I always keep the LORD in front of me.
  When he is by my side, I cannot be moved.
    That is why my heart is glad
      and my soul rejoices.
    My body rests securely.

Psalm 16:8-9

He will give you your heart's desire
  and carry out all your plans.

Psalm 20:4

The LORD advises those who fear him.
  He reveals to them the intent of his promise.

Psalm 25:14

When I was panic-stricken, I said,
  "I have been cut off from your sight."
But you heard my pleas for mercy
    when I cried out to you for help.

Psalm 31:22

  No harm will come to you.
  No sickness will come near your house.
He will put his angels in charge of you
  to protect you in all your ways.
    They will carry you in their hands

so that you never hit your foot against a rock.
You will step on lions and cobras.
You will trample young lions and snakes.

Psalm 91:10-13

I, the LORD your God, hold your right hand
and say to you, "Don't be afraid; I will help you."

Isaiah 41:13

Ask, and you will receive. Search, and you will find. Knock, and the door will be opened for you. Everyone who asks will receive. The one who searches will find, and for the one who knocks, the door will be opened.

Matthew 7:7-8

Jesus spoke to the Pharisees again. He said, "I am the light of the world. Whoever follows me will have a life filled with light and will never live in the dark."

John 8:12

Persecuted

Do not be afraid, because I have reclaimed you.
  I have called you by name; you are mine.
When you go through the sea, I am with you.
When you go through rivers, they will not sweep you
    away.
When you walk through fire, you will not be burned,
  and the flames will not harm you.

Isaiah 43:1-2

I have refined you,
  but not like silver.
I have tested you in the furnace of suffering.

Isaiah 48:10

Blessed are those who are persecuted
  for doing what God approves of.
  The kingdom of heaven belongs to them.

Blessed are you when people insult you,
  persecute you,
    lie, and say all kinds of evil things about you
      because of me.

Matthew 5:10-11

You have heard that it was said, "Love your neighbor, and
hate your enemy." But I tell you this: Love your enemies,
and pray for those who persecute you. In this way you

show that you are children of your Father in heaven. He makes his sun rise on people whether they are good or evil. He lets rain fall on them whether they are just or unjust. If you love those who love you, do you deserve a reward? Even the tax collectors do that! Are you doing anything remarkable if you welcome only your friends? Everyone does that! That is why you must be perfect as your Father in heaven is perfect.

Matthew 5:43-48

When you are put on trial in synagogues or in front of rulers and authorities, don't worry about how you will defend yourselves or what you will say. At that time the Holy Spirit will teach you what you must say.

Luke 12:11-12

If the world hates you, realize that it hated me before it hated you. If you had anything in common with the world, the world would love you as one of its own. But you don't have anything in common with the world. I chose you from the world, and that's why the world hates you.

John 15:18-19

But now, Father, I'm coming back to you. I say these things while I'm still in the world so that they will have the same joy that I have. I have given them your message. But the world has hated them because they don't belong to the world any more than I belong to the world. I'm not asking you to take them out of the world but to protect them from the evil one. They don't belong to the world any more than I belong to the world. Use the truth to make them holy. Your words are truth.

John 17:13-17

We also brag when we are suffering. We know that suffering creates endurance, endurance creates character, and character creates confidence. We're not ashamed to have this confidence, because God's love has been poured into our hearts by the Holy Spirit, who has been given to us.

Romans 5:3-5

Bless those who persecute you. Bless them, and don't curse them.

Romans 12:14

Don't let evil conquer you, but conquer evil with good.

Romans 12:21

In every way we're troubled, but we aren't crushed by our troubles. We're frustrated, but we don't give up. We're persecuted, but we're not abandoned. We're captured, but we're not killed.

2 Corinthians 4:8-9

All this is for your sake so that, as God's kindness overflows in the lives of many people, it will produce even more thanksgiving to the glory of God. That is why we are not discouraged. Though outwardly we are wearing out, inwardly we are renewed day by day. Our suffering is light and temporary and is producing for us an eternal glory that is greater than anything we can imagine. We don't look for things that can be seen but for things that can't be seen. Things that can be seen are only temporary. But things that can't be seen last forever.

2 Corinthians 4:15-18

Keep a clear head in everything. Endure suffering.

2 Timothy 4:5

My brothers and sisters, be very happy when you are tested in different ways. You know that such testing of your faith produces endurance. Endure until your testing is over. Then you will be mature and complete, and you won't need anything.

James 1:2-4

You are extremely happy about these things, even though you have to suffer different kinds of trouble for a little while now. The purpose of these troubles is to test your faith as fire tests how genuine gold is. Your faith is more precious than gold, and by passing the test, it gives praise, glory, and honor to God. This will happen when Jesus Christ appears again.

1 Peter 1:6-7

God called you to endure suffering because Christ suffered for you. He left you an example so that you could follow in his footsteps. Christ never committed any sin. He never spoke deceitfully. Christ never verbally abused those who verbally abused him. When he suffered, he didn't make any threats but left everything to the one who judges fairly.

1 Peter 2:21-23

Don't pay people back with evil for the evil they do to you, or ridicule those who ridicule you. Instead, bless them, because you were called to inherit a blessing.

1 Peter 3:9

Even if you suffer for doing what God approves, you are blessed. Don't be afraid of those who want to harm you. Don't get upset. But dedicate your lives to Christ as Lord. Always be ready to defend your confidence in God when anyone asks you to explain it. However, make your defense with gentleness and respect. Keep your conscience clear. Then those who treat the good Christian life you live with contempt will feel ashamed that they have ridiculed you. After all, if it is God's will, it's better to suffer for doing good than for doing wrong.

1 Peter 3:14-17

Since Christ has suffered physically, take the same attitude that he had. (A person who has suffered physically no longer sins.) That way you won't be guided by sinful human desires as you live the rest of your lives on earth. Instead, you will be guided by what God wants you to do.

1 Peter 4:1-2

Dear friends, don't be surprised by the fiery troubles that are coming in order to test you. Don't feel as though something strange is happening to you, but be happy as you share Christ's sufferings. Then you will also be full of joy when he appears again in his glory. If you are insulted because of the name of Christ, you are blessed because the Spirit of glory—the Spirit of God—is resting on you.

1 Peter 4:12-14

Rebellious

And now, Lord, what am I waiting for?
My hope is in you!
Rescue me from all my rebellious acts.
Do not disgrace me in front of godless fools.

Psalm 39:7-8

O LORD, set a guard at my mouth.
  Keep watch over the door of my lips.
  Do not let me be persuaded to do anything evil
    or to become involved with wickedness,
      with people who are troublemakers.
        Do not let me taste their delicacies.

Psalm 141:3-4

Remember your Creator before the sun, the light, the
    moon,
  and the stars turn dark, and the clouds come back
    with rain.
Remember your Creator when those who guard the
    house tremble,
  strong men are stooped over,
    the women at the mill stop grinding
      because there are so few of them,
        and those who look out of the windows
          see a dim light.
Remember your Creator when the doors to the street
    are closed,

the sound of the mill is muffled,
   you are startled at the sound of a bird,
      and those who sing songs become quiet.

Ecclesiastes 12:2-4

He was abused and punished,
   but he didn't open his mouth.
He was led like a lamb to the slaughter.
He was like a sheep that is silent
   when its wool is cut off.
      He didn't open his mouth.

He was arrested, taken away, and judged.
   Who would have thought that he would be removed
      from the world?
He was killed because of my people's rebellion.

Isaiah 53:7-8

Let's return to the LORD.
   Even though he has torn us to pieces,
      he will heal us.
   Even though he has wounded us,
      he will bandage our wounds.

Hosea 6:1

Then I will give all people pure lips
   to worship the LORD
      and to serve him with one purpose.
From beyond the rivers of Sudan
   my worshipers, my scattered people, will bring my
      offering.
On that day you will no longer be ashamed
   of all your rebellious acts against me.
Then I will remove your arrogance

and never again will you act proud on my holy
mountain.

Zephaniah 3:9-11

Then Jesus called the crowd to himself along with his disciples. He said to them, "Those who want to follow me must say no to the things they want, pick up their crosses, and follow me. Those who want to save their lives will lose them. But those who lose their lives for me and for the Good News will save them."

Mark 8:34-35

Whoever knows and obeys my commandments is the person who loves me. Those who love me will have my Father's love, and I, too, will love them and show myself to them.

John 14:21

Then Jesus said, "I am the true vine, and my Father takes care of the vineyard. He removes every one of my branches that doesn't produce fruit. He also prunes every branch that does produce fruit to make it produce more fruit."

John 15:1-2

Never offer any part of your body to sin's power. No part of your body should ever be used to do any ungodly thing. Instead, offer yourselves to God as people who have come back from death and are now alive. Offer all the parts of your body to God. Use them to do everything that God approves of. Certainly, sin shouldn't have power over you because you're not controlled by laws, but by God's favor.

Romans 6:13-14

You were slaves to sin. But I thank God that you have become wholeheartedly obedient to the teachings which you were given. Freed from sin, you were made slaves who do what God approves of.

Romans 6:17-18

Every person should obey the government in power. No government would exist if it hadn't been established by God. The governments which exist have been put in place by God. Therefore, whoever resists the government opposes what God has established. Those who resist will bring punishment on themselves.

Romans 13:1-2

So place yourselves under God's authority. Resist the devil, and he will run away from you. Come close to God, and he will come close to you.

James 4:7-8

Place yourselves under the authority of human governments to please the Lord. Obey the emperor. He holds the highest position of authority. Also obey governors. They are people the emperor has sent to punish those who do wrong and to praise those who do right.

1 Peter 2:13-14

To love God means that we obey his commandments. Obeying his commandments isn't difficult because everyone who has been born from God has won the victory over the world. Our faith is what wins the victory over the world. Who wins the victory over the world? Isn't it the person who believes that Jesus is the Son of God?

1 John 5:3-5

Sexually Wounded

I love you, O LORD, my strength.
The LORD is my rock and my fortress and my Savior,
   my God, my rock in whom I take refuge,
     my shield, and the strength of my salvation,
      my stronghold.

                           Psalm 18:1-2

The LORD is my strength and my shield.
My heart trusted him, so I received help.
My heart is triumphant;
   I give thanks to him with my song.

                           Psalm 28:7

Save your people, and bless those who belong to you.
Be their shepherd, and carry them forever.

                           Psalm 28:9

You have made me endure many terrible troubles.
You restore me to life again.
You bring me back from the depths of the earth.
You comfort me and make me greater than ever.

                           Psalm 71:20-21

You comfort me and make me greater than ever.

Because of your faithfulness, O my God,
even I will give thanks to you.

Psalm 71:21-22

O God, restore us and smile on us
so that we may be saved.

Psalm 80:3

The High and Lofty One lives forever, and his name is
holy.

This is what he says:

I live in a high and holy place.
But I am with those who are crushed and humble.
I will renew the spirit of those who are humble
and the courage of those who are crushed.

Isaiah 57:15

Tempted

Don't allow us to be tempted.
Instead, rescue us from the evil one.

Matthew 6:13

There isn't any temptation that you have experienced which is unusual for humans. God, who faithfully keeps his promises, will not allow you to be tempted beyond your power to resist. But when you are tempted, he will also give you the ability to endure the temptation as your way of escape.

1 Corinthians 10:13

We have a chief priest who is able to sympathize with our weaknesses. He was tempted in every way that we are, but he didn't sin. So we can go confidently to the throne of God's kindness to receive mercy and find kindness, which will help us at the right time.

Hebrews 4:15-16

Waiting

Wait with hope for the LORD.
Be strong, and let your heart be courageous.
Yes, wait with hope for the LORD.

Psalm 27:14

I waited patiently for the LORD.
  He turned to me and heard my cry for help.
  He pulled me out of a horrible pit,
    out of the mud and clay.
  He set my feet on a rock
    and made my steps secure.
  He placed a new song in my mouth,
    a song of praise to our God.
      Many will see this and worship.
      They will trust the LORD.
Blessed is the person
  who places his confidence in the LORD
    and does not rely on arrogant people
      or those who follow lies.

Psalm 40:1-4

My soul waits calmly for God alone.
  My salvation comes from him.
He alone is my rock and my savior—my stronghold.
  I cannot be severely shaken.

Psalm 62:1-2

Do not let those who wait with hope for you
  be put to shame because of me,

O Almighty LORD of Armies.
Do not let those who come to you for help
 be humiliated because of me, O God of Israel.

Psalm 69:6

I wait for the LORD, my soul waits,
 and with hope I wait for his word.
My soul waits for the LORD
 more than those who watch for the morning,
 more than those who watch for the morning.

Psalm 130:5-6

The LORD is pleased with those who fear him,
 with those who wait with hope for his mercy.

Psalm 147:11

The path of the righteous is level.
 O Upright One, you make the road of the righteous
  smooth.
Certainly, we wait with hope for you, O LORD,
 as we follow the path of your guiding principles.
 We want to remember you and your name.

Isaiah 26:7-8

O LORD, have pity on us.
 We wait with hope for you.
Be our strength in the morning.
 Yes, be our savior in times of trouble.

Isaiah 33:2

Yet, the strength of those who wait with hope in the LORD
 will be renewed.
  They will soar on wings like eagles.
  They will run and won't become weary.
  They will walk and won't grow tired.

Isaiah 40:31

When You Can't Stop . . .

Doubting God

However, if my people, who are called by my name,
     will humble themselves,
       pray, search for me, and turn from their evil ways,
then I will hear their prayer from heaven, forgive their
     sins,
       and heal their country.

2 Chronicles 7:14

Trust the LORD, and do good things.
Live in the land, and practice being faithful.
Be happy with the LORD,
     and he will give you the desires of your heart.
Entrust your ways to the LORD.
Trust him, and he will act on your behalf.

Psalm 37:3-5

The LORD God is a sun and shield.
The LORD grants favor and honor.
He does not hold back any blessing
     from those who live innocently.

O LORD of Armies, blessed is the person
     who trusts you.

Psalm 84:11-12

Shout happily to the LORD, all the earth.
Serve the LORD cheerfully.

Come into his presence with a joyful song.
Realize that the LORD alone is God.
He made us, and we are his.
We are his people and the sheep in his care.
Enter his gates with a song of thanksgiving.
Come into his courtyards with a song of praise.
Give thanks to him; praise his name.
The LORD is good.
His mercy endures forever.
His faithfulness endures
throughout every generation.

Psalm 100

Praise the LORD, all you nations!
Praise him, all you people of the world!
His mercy toward us is powerful.
The LORD's faithfulness endures forever.

Hallelujah!

Psalm 117

Those who trust the LORD are like Mount Zion,
which can never be shaken.
It remains firm forever.
As the mountains surround Jerusalem,
so the LORD surrounds his people now and forever.

Psalm 125:1-2

Trust the LORD with all your heart,
and do not rely on your own understanding.
In all your ways acknowledge him,
and he will make your paths smooth.

Proverbs 3:5-6

Entrust your efforts to the LORD,
   and your plans will succeed.
                    Proverbs 16:3

The king's heart is like streams of water.
   Both are under the LORD's control.
      He turns them in any direction he chooses.
                    Proverbs 21:1

It is beautiful how God has done everything at the right time. He has put a sense of eternity in people's minds.
                    Ecclesiastes 3:11

In the year King Uzziah died, I saw the Lord sitting on a high and lofty throne. The bottom of his robe filled the temple. Angels were standing above him. Each had six wings: With two they covered their faces, with two they covered their feet, and with two they flew. They called to each other and said,

   "Holy, holy, holy is the LORD of Armies!
   The whole earth is filled with his glory."
                    Isaiah 6:1-3

This is what the Almighty LORD, the Holy One of Israel, says:

   You can be saved by returning to me.
   You can have rest.
   You can be strong by being quiet and by trusting me.
      But you don't want that.

                    Isaiah 30:15

Jesus and his disciples went to the villages around Caesarea Philippi. On the way he asked his disciples, "Who do people say I am?" They answered him, "Some say you are John the Baptizer, others Elijah, still others one of the prophets." He asked them, "But who do you say I am?" Peter answered him, "You are the Messiah!"

Mark 8:27-29

Then Jesus said to the disciples, "Have faith in God. I tell you the truth, you can say to this mountain, 'May you be lifted up and thrown into the sea,' and it will happen. But you must really believe it will happen and have no doubt in your heart. I tell you, you can pray for anything, and if you believe that you've received it, it will be yours."

Mark 11:22-24

The apostles said to the Lord, "Give us more faith." The Lord said, "If you have faith the size of a mustard seed, you could say to this mulberry tree, 'Pull yourself up by the roots, and plant yourself in the sea!' and it would obey you."

Luke 17:5-6

I can guarantee this truth: Those who believe in me will do the things that I am doing. They will do even greater things because I am going to the Father. I will do anything you ask the Father in my name so that the Father will be given glory because of the Son. If you ask me to do something, I will do it.

John 14:12-14

Jesus performed many other miracles that his disciples saw. Those miracles are not written in this book. But these miracles have been written so that you will believe that

Jesus is the Messiah, the Son of God, and so that you will have life by believing in him.

John 20:30-31

Our lives are guided by faith, not by sight.

2 Corinthians 5:7

He is far above all rulers, authorities, powers, lords, and all other names that can be named, not only in this present world but also in the world to come. God has put everything under the control of Christ. He has made Christ the head of everything for the good of the church. The church is Christ's body and completes him as he fills everything in every way.

Ephesians 2:21-23

His Son is the reflection of God's glory and the exact likeness of God's being. He holds everything together through his powerful words. After he had cleansed people from their sins, he received the highest position, the one next to the Father in heaven.

Hebrews 1:3

Jesus Christ is the same yesterday, today, and forever.

Hebrews 13:8

Doubting Others

Even my closest friend whom I trusted,
   the one who ate my bread,
      has lifted his heel against me.
Have pity on me, O Lord!
Raise me up so that I can pay them back.
Psalm 41:9-10

You saved me from death.
You saved my eyes from tears
   and my feet from stumbling.
I will walk in the Lord's presence in this world
   of the living.
I kept my faith even when I said,
   "I am suffering terribly."
I also said when I was panic-stricken,
   "Everyone is undependable."
How can I repay the Lord
   for all the good that he has done for me?
Psalm 116:8-12

Wives, place yourselves under your husbands' authority as you have placed yourselves under the Lord's authority. The husband is the head of his wife as Christ is the head of the church. It is his body, and he is its Savior. As the church is under Christ's authority, so wives are under their husbands' authority in everything.

Husbands, love your wives as Christ loved the church and gave his life for it. He did this to make the church holy by cleansing it, washing it using water along with spoken words. Then he could present it to himself as a glorious church, without any kind of stain or wrinkle—holy and without faults. So husbands must love their wives as they love their own bodies. A man who loves his wife loves himself.

Ephesians 5:22-28

Children, obey your parents because you are Christians. This is the right thing to do. "Honor your father and mother that everything may go well for you, and you may have a long life on earth." This is an important commandment with a promise.

Ephesians 6:1-3

Whatever you do, do it wholeheartedly as though you were working for your real master and not merely for humans.

Colossians 3:23

Drinking

We should live decently, as people who live in the light of day. Wild parties, drunkenness, sexual immorality, promiscuity, rivalry, and jealousy cannot be part of our lives. Instead, live like the Lord Jesus Christ did, and forget about satisfying the desires of your sinful nature.

Romans 13:13-14

What your corrupt nature wants is contrary to what your spiritual nature wants, and what your spiritual nature wants is contrary to what your corrupt nature wants. They are opposed to each other. As a result, you don't always do what you intend to do. . . . Now, the effects of the corrupt nature are obvious: illicit sex, perversion, promiscuity, idolatry, drug use, hatred, rivalry, jealousy, angry outbursts, selfish ambition, conflict, factions, envy, drunkenness, wild partying, and things like that. I've told you in the past and I'm telling you again that people who do things like that will not inherit the kingdom of God. But the spiritual nature produces love, joy, peace, patience, kindness, goodness, faithfulness, gentleness, and self-control. There are no laws against things like that. Those who belong to Christ Jesus have crucified their corrupt nature along with its passions and desires. If we live by our spiritual nature, then our lives need to conform to our spiritual nature.

Galatians 5:17-25

Don't get drunk on wine, which leads to wild living. Instead, be filled with the Spirit by reciting psalms, hymns, and spiritual songs for your own good. Sing and make music to the Lord with your hearts. Always thank God the Father for everything in the name of our Lord Jesus Christ. Place yourselves under each other's authority out of respect for Christ.

Ephesians 5:18-21

Feeling Guilty

Have pity on me, O LORD, because I am in distress.
   My eyes, my soul, and my body
      waste away from grief.
   My life is exhausted from sorrow,
      my years from groaning.
   My strength staggers under the weight of my guilt,
      and my bones waste away.

                                        Psalm 31:9-10

You removed your people's guilt.
You pardoned all their sins. *Selah*

                        Psalm 85:2

"Comfort my people! Comfort them!" says your God.
"Speak tenderly to Jerusalem and announce to it
   that its time of hard labor is over
      and its wrongs have been paid for.
         It has received from the LORD double for all
            its sins."

                              Isaiah 40:1-2

So I've discovered this truth: Evil is present with me even
when I want to do what God's standards say is good. I take
pleasure in God's standards in my inner being. However, I
see a different standard at work throughout my body. It is
at war with the standards my mind sets and tries to take

me captive to sin's standards which still exist throughout my body. What a miserable person I am! Who will rescue me from my dying body? I thank God that our Lord Jesus Christ rescues me! So I am obedient to God's standards with my mind, but I am obedient to sin's standards with my corrupt nature.

Romans 7:21-25

The one who loves us gives us an overwhelming victory in all these difficulties. I am convinced that nothing can ever separate us from God's love which Christ Jesus our Lord shows us. We can't be separated by death or life, by angels or rulers, by anything in the present or anything in the future, by forces or powers in the world above or in the world below, or by anything else in creation.

Romans 8:37-39

God is faithful and reliable. If we confess our sins, he forgives them and cleanses us from everything we've done wrong.

1 John 1:9

Grieving

(You have kept a record of my wanderings.
   Put my tears in your bottle.
      They are already in your book.)
Then my enemies will retreat when I call to you.
This I know: God is on my side.

Psalm 56:8-9

Precious in the sight of the LORD
   is the death of his faithful ones.

Psalm 116:15

I am drowning in tears.
   Strengthen me as you promised.

Psalm 119:28

Blessed are those who mourn.
   They will be comforted.

Matthew 5:4

Jesus said to her, "I am the one who brings people back to life, and I am life itself. Those who believe in me will live even if they die. Everyone who lives and believes in me will never die."

John 11:25-26

Jesus knew they wanted to ask him something. So he said to them, "Are you trying to figure out among yourselves what I meant when I said, 'In a little while you won't see me, and in a little while you will see me again'? I can guarantee this truth: You will cry because you are sad, but the world will be happy. You will feel pain, but your pain will turn to happiness. A woman has pain when her time to give birth comes. But after the child is born, she doesn't remember the pain anymore because she's happy that a child has been brought into the world. Now you're in a painful situation. But I will see you again. Then you will be happy, and no one will take that happiness away from you."

John 16:19-22

Brothers and sisters, we don't want you to be ignorant about those who have died. We don't want you to grieve like other people who have no hope. We believe that Jesus died and came back to life. We also believe that, through Jesus, God will bring back those who have died. They will come back with Jesus.

1 Thessalonians 4:13-14

I saw a new heaven and a new earth, because the first heaven and earth had disappeared, and the sea was gone. Then I saw the holy city, New Jerusalem, coming down from God out of heaven, dressed like a bride ready for her husband. I heard a loud voice from the throne say, "God lives with humans! God will make his home with them, and they will be his people. God himself will be with them and be their God. He will wipe every tear from their eyes. There won't be any more death. There won't be any grief, crying, or pain, because the first things have disappeared."

Revelation 21:1-4

Hurting Yourself

Have pity on me, O LORD, because I am weak.
Heal me, O LORD, because my bones shake
    with terror.

Psalm 6:2

The LORD is a stronghold for the oppressed,
    a stronghold in times of trouble.
Those who know your name trust you, O LORD,
    because you have never deserted
        those who seek your help.

Psalm 9:9-10

I, the LORD, have called you to do what is right.
    I will take hold of your hand.
    I will protect you.
    I will appoint you as my promise to the people,
        as my light to the nations.

Isaiah 42:6

Who among you fears the LORD
    and obeys his servant?
Let those who walk in darkness and have no light
    trust the name of the LORD
        and depend upon their God.

Isaiah 50:10

The Spirit of the Almighty LORD is with me
because the LORD has anointed me
to deliver good news to humble people.
He has sent me
to heal those who are brokenhearted,
to announce that captives will be set free
and prisoners will be released.

Isaiah 61:1

Heal me, O LORD, and I will be healed.
Rescue me, and I will be rescued.
You are the one I praise.

Jeremiah 17:14

Don't you know that your body is a temple that belongs to the Holy Spirit? The Holy Spirit, whom you received from God, lives in you. You don't belong to yourselves. You were bought for a price. So bring glory to God in the way you use your body.

1 Corinthians 6:19-20

I thank God, who always leads us in victory because of Christ.

2 Corinthians 2:14

Keep your mind clear, and be alert. Your opponent the devil is prowling around like a roaring lion as he looks for someone to devour. Be firm in the faith and resist him, knowing that other believers throughout the world are going through the same kind of suffering.

1 Peter 5:8-9

Judging Others

Stop judging so that you will not be judged. Otherwise, you will be judged by the same standard you use to judge others. The standards you use for others will be applied to you. So why do you see the piece of sawdust in another believer's eye and not notice the wooden beam in your own eye? How can you say to another believer, "Let me take the piece of sawdust out of your eye," when you have a beam in your own eye? You hypocrite! First remove the beam from your own eye. Then you will see clearly to remove the piece of sawdust from another believer's eye.

Matthew 7:1-5

Welcome people who are weak in faith, but don't get into an argument over differences of opinion. Some people believe that they can eat all kinds of food. Other people with weak faith believe that they can eat only vegetables. People who eat all foods should not despise people who eat only vegetables. In the same way, the vegetarians should not criticize people who eat all foods, because God has accepted those people.

Romans 14:1-3

Help carry each other's burdens. In this way you will follow Christ's teachings.

Galatians 6:2

Imitate God, since you are the children he loves. Live in love as Christ also loved us. He gave his life for us as an offering and sacrifice, a soothing aroma to God.

Ephesians 5:1-2

As holy people whom God has chosen and loved, be sympathetic, kind, humble, gentle, and patient. Put up with each other, and forgive each other if anyone has a complaint. Forgive as the Lord forgave you. Above all, be loving. This ties everything together perfectly. Also, let Christ's peace control you. God has called you into this peace by bringing you into one body. Be thankful.

Colossians 3:12-15

Remember this, my dear brothers and sisters: Everyone should be quick to listen, slow to speak, and should not get angry easily.

James 1:19

When You Need . . .

To Comfort Others

Then Job replied to his friends,

"Listen carefully to my words,
  and let that be the comfort you offer me."
                                              Job 21:1-2

A person's anxiety will weigh him down,
  but an encouraging word makes him joyful.
                                              Proverbs 12:25

A friend always loves,
  and a brother is born to share trouble.
                                              Proverbs 17:17

Friends can destroy one another,
  but a loving friend can stick closer than family.
                                              Proverbs 18:24

Like golden apples in silver settings,
  so is a word spoken at the right time.
Like a gold ring and a fine gold ornament,
  so is constructive criticism to the ear of one
    who listens.
                                              Proverbs 25:11-12

The Almighty LORD will teach me what to say,
  so I will know how to encourage weary people.

Morning after morning he will wake me
    to listen like a student.

Isaiah 50:4

Be careful not to do your good works in public in order to
attract attention. If you do, your Father in heaven will not
reward you. So when you give to the poor, don't announce
it with trumpet fanfare. This is what hypocrites do in the
synagogues and on the streets in order to be praised by
people. I can guarantee this truth: That will be their only
reward. When you give to the poor, don't let your left hand
know what your right hand is doing. Give your contribu-
tions privately. Your Father sees what you do in private.
He will reward you.

Matthew 6:1-4

The person who welcomes you welcomes me, and the person who welcomes me welcomes the one who sent me.

Matthew 10:40

I can guarantee this truth: Whoever gives any of my humble
followers a cup of cold water because that person is my
disciple will certainly never lose his reward.

Matthew 10:42

When the Pharisees heard that Jesus had silenced the Sad-
ducees, they gathered together. One of them, an expert in
Moses' Teachings, tested Jesus by asking, "Teacher, which
commandment is the greatest in Moses' Teachings?" Jesus
answered him, "'Love the Lord your God with all your
heart, with all your soul, and with all your mind.' This
is the greatest and most important commandment. The
second is like it: 'Love your neighbor as you love yourself.'
All of Moses' Teachings and the Prophets depend on these
two commandments."

Matthew 22:34-40

Give, and you will receive. A large quantity, pressed together, shaken down, and running over will be put into your pocket. The standards you use for others will be applied to you.

Luke 6:38

After Jesus had washed their feet and put on his outer clothes, he took his place at the table again. Then he asked his disciples, "Do you understand what I've done for you? You call me teacher and Lord, and you're right because that's what I am. So if I, your Lord and teacher, have washed your feet, you must wash each other's feet. I've given you an example that you should follow. I can guarantee this truth: Slaves are not superior to their owners, and messengers are not superior to the people who send them. If you understand all of this, you are blessed whenever you follow my example."

John 13:12-17

Jesus' mother, her sister, Mary (the wife of Clopas), and Mary from Magdala were standing beside Jesus' cross. Jesus saw his mother and the disciple whom he loved standing there. He said to his mother, "Look, here's your son!" Then he said to the disciple, "Look, here's your mother!" From that time on she lived with that disciple in his home.

John 19:25-27

Love sincerely. Hate evil. Hold on to what is good. Be devoted to each other like a loving family. Excel in showing respect for each other. Don't be lazy in showing your devotion. Use your energy to serve the Lord.

Romans 12:9-11

Be happy in your confidence, be patient in trouble, and pray continually.

Romans 12:12

Share what you have with God's people who are in need. Be hospitable.

Romans 12:13

Be happy with those who are happy. Be sad with those who are sad.

Romans 12:15

The commandments, "Never commit adultery; never murder; never steal; never have wrong desires," and every other commandment are summed up in this statement: "Love your neighbor as you love yourself." Love never does anything that is harmful to a neighbor. Therefore, love fulfills Moses' Teachings.

Romans 13:9-10

So let's pursue those things which bring peace and which are good for each other.

Romans 14:19

May God, who gives you this endurance and encouragement, allow you to live in harmony with each other by following the example of Christ Jesus. Then, having the same goal, you will praise the God and Father of our Lord Jesus Christ.

Romans 15:5-6

Therefore, accept each other in the same way that Christ accepted you. He did this to bring glory to God.

Romans 15:7

Be careful that by using your freedom you don't somehow make a believer who is weak in faith fall into sin.

1 Corinthians 8:9

So, whether you eat or drink, or whatever you do, do everything to the glory of God. Don't cause others to stumble.

1 Corinthians 10:31-32

God has put the body together and given special honor to the part that doesn't have it. God's purpose was that the body should not be divided but rather that all of its parts should feel the same concern for each other. If one part of the body suffers, all the other parts share its suffering. If one part is praised, all the others share in its happiness.

1 Corinthians 12:24-26

Love is patient. Love is kind. Love isn't jealous. It doesn't sing its own praises. It isn't arrogant. It isn't rude. It doesn't think about itself. It isn't irritable. It doesn't keep track of wrongs. It isn't happy when injustice is done, but it is happy with the truth. Love never stops being patient, never stops believing, never stops hoping, never gives up. Love never comes to an end.

1 Corinthians 13:4-8

When a person speaks in another language, he doesn't speak to people but to God. No one understands him. His spirit is speaking mysteries. But when a person speaks what God has revealed, he speaks to people to help them grow, to encourage them, and to comfort them.

1 Corinthians 14:1-3

Because Christ suffered so much for us, we can receive so much comfort from him. Besides, if we suffer, it brings you comfort and salvation. If we are comforted, we can effectively comfort you when you endure the same sufferings that we endure. We have confidence in you. We know that as you share our sufferings, you also share our comfort.

2 Corinthians 1:5-6

Wherever we go, God uses us to make clear what it means to know Christ. It's like a fragrance that fills the air. To God we are the aroma of Christ among those who are saved and among those who are dying. To some people we are a deadly fragrance, while to others we are a life-giving fragrance.

2 Corinthians 2:14-16

Remember this: The farmer who plants a few seeds will have a very small harvest. But the farmer who plants because he has received God's blessings will receive a harvest of God's blessings in return. Each of you should give whatever you have decided. You shouldn't be sorry that you gave or feel forced to give, since God loves a cheerful giver. Besides, God will give you his constantly overflowing kindness. Then, when you always have everything you need, you can do more and more good things. Scripture says,

"The righteous person gives freely to the poor.
His righteousness continues forever."

2 Corinthians 9:6-9

Accept my encouragement. Share the same attitude and live in peace. The God of love and peace will be with you.

2 Corinthians 13:11

Brothers and sisters, if a person gets trapped by wrongdoing, those of you who are spiritual should help that person turn away from doing wrong. Do it in a gentle way. At the same time watch yourself so that you also are not tempted.

Galatians 6:1

Instead, as we lovingly speak the truth, we will grow up completely in our relationship to Christ, who is the head.

Ephesians 4:15

Don't say anything that would hurt another person. Instead, speak only what is good so that you can give help wherever it is needed. That way, what you say will help those who hear you. . . . Be kind to each other, sympathetic, forgiving each other as God has forgiven you through Christ.

Ephesians 4:29, 32

So then, as Christians, do you have any encouragement? Do you have any comfort from love? Do you have any spiritual relationships? Do you have any sympathy and compassion? Then fill me with joy by having the same attitude and the same love, living in harmony, and keeping one purpose in mind.

Philippians 2:1-2

Let everyone know how considerate you are. The Lord is near.

Philippians 4:5

Be wise in the way you act toward those who are outside the Christian faith. Make the most of your opportunities. Everything you say should be kind and well thought out so that you know how to answer everyone.

Colossians 4:5-6

Therefore, encourage each other and strengthen one another as you are doing.

1 Thessalonians 5:11

We encourage you, brothers and sisters, to instruct those who are not living right, cheer up those who are discouraged, help the weak, and be patient with everyone.

1 Thessalonians 5:14

Don't let anyone look down on you for being young. Instead, make your speech, behavior, love, faith, and purity an example for other believers.

1 Timothy 4:12

So, because we're brothers in the Lord, do something for me. Give me some comfort because of Christ. I am confident as I write to you that you will do this. And I know that you will do even more than I ask.

Philemon 20-21

You are doing right if you obey this law from the highest authority: "Love your neighbor as you love yourself." If you favor one person over another, you're sinning, and this law convicts you of being disobedient.

James 2:8-9

My brothers and sisters, what good does it do if someone claims to have faith but doesn't do any good things? Can this kind of faith save him? Suppose a believer, whether a man or a woman, needs clothes or food and one of you tells that person, "God be with you! Stay warm, and make sure you eat enough." If you don't provide for that person's physical needs, what good does it do? In the same way, faith by itself is dead if it doesn't cause you to do any good things.

James 2:14-17

Love each other with a warm love that comes from the heart. After all, you have purified yourselves by obeying the truth. As a result you have a sincere love for each other.

1 Peter 1:22

Each of you as a good manager must use the gift that God has given you to serve others. Whoever speaks must speak God's words. Whoever serves must serve with the strength God supplies so that in every way God receives glory through Jesus Christ. Glory and power belong to Jesus Christ forever and ever! Amen.

1 Peter 4:10-11

Dear children, we must show love through actions that are sincere, not through empty words.

1 John 3:18

Dear friends, we must love each other because love comes from God. Everyone who loves has been born from God and knows God.

1 John 4:7

Show mercy to those who have doubts.

Jude 22

Dignity/Worth

O LORD, look how my enemies have increased!
Many are attacking me.
Many are saying about me,
   "Even with God on his side,
      he won't be victorious." *Selah*

But you, O LORD, are a shield that surrounds me.
You are my glory.
You hold my head high.

Psalm 3:1-3

O God, you have heard my vows.
   You have given me the inheritance
      that belongs to those who fear your name.

Psalm 61:5

So I tell you to stop worrying about what you will eat,
drink, or wear. Isn't life more than food and the body more
than clothes? Look at the birds. They don't plant, harvest,
or gather the harvest into barns. Yet, your heavenly Father
feeds them. Aren't you worth more than they?

Matthew 6:25-26

He also gave apostles, prophets, missionaries, as well as
pastors and teachers as gifts to his church. Their purpose
is to prepare God's people, to serve, and to build up the

111

body of Christ. This is to continue until all of us are united in our faith and in our knowledge about God's Son, until we become mature, until we measure up to Christ, who is the standard.

Ephesians 4:11-13

What is a mortal that you should remember him,
 or the Son of Man that you take care of him?
You made him a little lower than the angels.
You crowned him with glory and honor.
You put everything under his control.

Hebrews 2:6-8

Consider this: The Father has given us his love. He loves us so much that we are actually called God's dear children. And that's what we are. For this reason the world doesn't recognize us, and it didn't recognize him either. Dear friends, now we are God's children. What we will be isn't completely clear yet. We do know that when Christ appears we will be like him because we will see him as he is.

1 John 3:1-2

Discipline

O LORD, blessed is the person
  whom you discipline and instruct
    from your teachings.
      You give him peace and quiet from times
        of trouble
        while a pit is dug to trap wicked people.

The LORD will never desert his people
  or abandon those who belong to him.

Psalm 94:12-14

A gracious woman wins respect,
  but ruthless men gain riches.
A merciful person helps himself,
  but a cruel person hurts himself.

Proverbs 11:16-17

The fear of the LORD is a fountain of life
  to turn one away from the grasp of death.

Proverbs 14:27

Whoever guards his mouth and his tongue
  keeps himself out of trouble.

Proverbs 21:23

Be ready for action, and have your lamps burning. Be like servants waiting to open the door at their master's knock when he returns from a wedding. Blessed are those servants whom the master finds awake when he comes. I can guarantee this truth: He will change his clothes, make them sit down at the table, and serve them. They will be blessed if he comes in the middle of the night or toward morning and finds them awake.

Luke 12:35-38

Endure your discipline. God corrects you as a father corrects his children. All children are disciplined by their fathers. If you aren't disciplined like the other children, you aren't part of the family.

Hebrews 12:7-8

On earth we have fathers who disciplined us, and we respect them. Shouldn't we place ourselves under the authority of God, the father of spirits, so that we will live? For a short time our fathers disciplined us as they thought best. Yet, God disciplines us for our own good so that we can become holy like him. We don't enjoy being disciplined. It always seems to cause more pain than joy. But later on, those who learn from that discipline have peace that comes from doing what is right.

Hebrews 12:9-11

Therefore, your minds must be clear and ready for action. Place your confidence completely in what God's kindness will bring you when Jesus Christ appears again. Because you are children who obey God, don't live the kind of lives you once lived. Once you lived to satisfy your desires because you didn't know any better. But because the God who called you is holy you must be holy in every aspect of your life. Scripture says, "Be holy, because I am holy."

1 Peter 1:13-16

Forgiveness

The LORD came down in a cloud and stood there with him and called out his name "the LORD." Then he passed in front of Moses, calling out, "The LORD, the LORD, a compassionate and merciful God, patient, always faithful and ready to forgive. He continues to show his love to thousands of generations, forgiving wrongdoing, disobedience, and sin. He never lets the guilty go unpunished, punishing children and grandchildren for their parents' sins to the third and fourth generation."

Exodus 34:5-7

Blessed is the person whose disobedience is forgiven
  and whose sin is pardoned.
Blessed is the person whom the LORD no longer
    accuses of sin
  and who has no deceitful thoughts.

Psalm 32:1-2

Have pity on me, O God, in keeping with your mercy.
  In keeping with your unlimited compassion,
    wipe out my rebellious acts.
Wash me thoroughly from my guilt,
  and cleanse me from my sin.
    I admit that I am rebellious.
    My sin is always in front of me.
I have sinned against you, especially you.
I have done what you consider evil.

So you hand down justice when you speak,
and you are blameless when you judge.

Create a clean heart in me, O God,
and renew a faithful spirit within me.

Psalm 51:1-4, 10

You, O Lord, are good and forgiving,
full of mercy toward everyone who calls out to you.
Open your ears to my prayer, O LORD.
Pay attention when I plead for mercy.
When I am in trouble, I call out to you
because you answer me.

Psalm 86:5-7

But you, O Lord, are a compassionate
and merciful God.
You are patient, always faithful and ready to forgive.

Psalm 86:15

Praise the LORD, my soul!
Praise his holy name, all that is within me.
Praise the LORD, my soul,
and never forget all the good he has done:
He is the one who forgives all your sins,
the one who heals all your diseases,
the one who rescues your life from the pit,
the one who crowns you
with mercy and compassion,
the one who fills your life with blessings
so that you become young again
like an eagle.

Psalm 103:1-5

So the LORD will comfort Zion.
He will comfort all those who live among its ruins.
He will make its desert like Eden.

He will make its wilderness like the garden of the
    LORD.
    Joy and gladness will be found in it,
        thanksgiving and the sound of singing.

Isaiah 51:3

I've seen their sinful ways, but I'll heal them.
I'll guide them and give them rest.
I'll comfort them and their mourners.

Isaiah 57:18

Their lives will be like well-watered gardens,
    and they will never suffer again.
Then young women will rejoice and dance
    along with young men and old men.
I will turn their mourning into joy.
I will comfort them.
I will give them joy in place of their sorrow.

Jeremiah 31:12-13

Then Peter came to Jesus and asked him, "Lord, how often
do I have to forgive a believer who wrongs me? Seven times?"
Jesus answered him, "I tell you, not just seven times, but
seventy times seven."

Matthew 18:21-22

If someone caused distress, I'm not the one really affected.
To some extent—although I don't want to emphasize this
too much—it has affected all of you. The majority of
you have imposed a severe enough punishment on that
person. So now forgive and comfort him. Such distress
could overwhelm someone like that if he's not forgiven
and comforted. That is why I urge you to assure him that
you love him.

2 Corinthians 2:5-8

Humility

The LORD told Samuel, "Don't look at his appearance or how tall he is, because I have rejected him. God does not see as humans see. Humans look at outward appearances, but the LORD looks into the heart."

1 Samuel 16:7

At that time the disciples came to Jesus and asked, "Who is greatest in the kingdom of heaven?"

He called a little child and had him stand among them. Then he said to them, "I can guarantee this truth: Unless you change and become like little children, you will never enter the kingdom of heaven. Whoever becomes like this little child is the greatest in the kingdom of heaven."

Matthew 18:1-4

The person who is greatest among you will be your servant. Whoever honors himself will be humbled, and whoever humbles himself will be honored.

Matthew 23:11-12

On a day of worship Jesus went to eat at the home of a prominent Pharisee. The guests were watching Jesus very closely. . . .

Then Jesus noticed how the guests always chose the places of honor. So he used this illustration when he spoke to them: "When someone invites you to a wedding, don't take the place of honor. Maybe someone more important than you was invited. Then your host would say to you, 'Give this person your place.' Embarrassed, you would have to take the place of least honor. So when you're invited, take the place of least honor. Then, when your host comes, he will tell you, 'Friend, move to a more honorable place.' Then all the other guests will see how you are honored. Those who honor themselves will be humbled, but people who humble themselves will be honored."

Luke 14:1, 7-11

Jesus also used this illustration with some who were sure that God approved of them while they looked down on everyone else. He said, "Two men went into the temple courtyard to pray. One was a Pharisee, and the other was a tax collector. The Pharisee stood up and prayed, 'God, I thank you that I'm not like other people! I'm not a robber or a dishonest person. I haven't committed adultery. I'm not even like this tax collector. I fast twice a week, and I give you a tenth of my entire income.'

"But the tax collector was standing at a distance. He wouldn't even look up to heaven. Instead, he became very upset, and he said, 'God, be merciful to me, a sinner!'

"I can guarantee that this tax collector went home with God's approval, but the Pharisee didn't. Everyone who honors himself will be humbled, but the person who humbles himself will be honored."

Luke 18:9-14

Young people, in a similar way, place yourselves under the authority of spiritual leaders. Furthermore, all of you must serve each other with humility, because God opposes the arrogant but favors the humble.

1 Peter 5:5

Joy

Don't be sad because the joy you have in the LORD is your strength.

Nehemiah 8:10

Let the light of your presence shine on us, O LORD.
    You put more joy in my heart
        than when their grain and new wine increase.
I fall asleep in peace the moment I lie down
    because you alone, O LORD, enable me
        to live securely.

Psalm 4:6-8

You have changed my sobbing into dancing.
You have removed my sackcloth and clothed me
    with joy
  so that my soul may praise you
    with music and not be silent.
O LORD my God, I will give thanks to you forever.

Psalm 30:11-12

Righteous people will find joy in the LORD
    and take refuge in him.
Everyone whose motives are decent
    will be able to brag.

Psalm 64:10

The LORD has done spectacular things for us.
    We are overjoyed.
Restore our fortunes, O LORD,
    as you restore streams to dry riverbeds in the Negev.
Those who cry while they plant
    will joyfully sing while they harvest.
The person who goes out weeping,
      carrying his bag of seed,
    will come home singing, carrying his bundles
        of grain.

Psalm 126:3-6

The fear of the LORD lengthens the number of days,
    but the years of wicked people are shortened.
The hope of righteous people leads to joy,
    but the eager waiting of wicked people comes
      to nothing.

Proverbs 10:27-28

Break out into shouts of joy, ruins of Jerusalem.
    The LORD will comfort his people.
      He will reclaim Jerusalem.

Isaiah 52:9

You will go out with joy and be led out in peace.
    The mountains and the hills
      will break into songs of joy in your presence,
        and all the trees will clap their hands.

Isaiah 55:12

I will find joy in the LORD.
I will delight in my God.
    He has dressed me in the clothes of salvation.
    He has wrapped me in the robe of righteousness

like a bridegroom with a priest's turban,
like a bride with her jewels.

Isaiah 61:10

I will create a new heaven and a new earth.
Past things will not be remembered.
They will not come to mind.
Be glad, and rejoice forever in what I'm going to create,
because I'm going to create Jerusalem to be a delight
and its people to be a joy.

Isaiah 65:17-18

I have loved you the same way the Father has loved me. So live in my love. If you obey my commandments, you will live in my love. I have obeyed my Father's commandments, and in that way I live in his love. I have told you this so that you will be as joyful as I am, and your joy will be complete.

John 15:9-11

Always be joyful in the Lord! I'll say it again: Be joyful!

Philippians 4:4

Always be joyful. Never stop praying. Whatever happens, give thanks, because it is God's will in Christ Jesus that you do this.

1 Thessalonians 5:16-18

Justice

The LORD judges the people of the world.
Judge me, O LORD,
    according to my righteousness,
    according to my integrity.

My shield is God above,
    who saves those whose motives are decent.
Psalm 7:8, 10

Yet, the LORD is enthroned forever.
    He has set up his throne for judgment.
    He alone judges the world with righteousness.
    He judges its people fairly.
Psalm 9:7-8

You have heard the desire of oppressed people,
    O LORD.
You encourage them.
You pay close attention to them
    in order to provide justice for orphans
        and oppressed people
        so that no mere mortal will terrify them again.
Psalm 10:17-18

The LORD loves justice,
    and he will not abandon his godly ones.

They will be kept safe forever,
  but the descendants of wicked people
    will be cut off.

Psalm 37:28

Judge me, O God,
  and plead my case against an ungodly nation.
Rescue me from deceitful and unjust people.

Send your light and your truth.
  Let them guide me.
  Let them bring me to your holy mountain
    and to your dwelling place.

Psalm 43:1-3

God alone is the judge.
  He punishes one person and rewards another.
A cup is in the LORD's hand.
  (Its foaming wine is thoroughly mixed with spices.)
He will empty it,
  and all the wicked people on earth
    will have to drink every last drop.

Psalm 75:7-8

Let the rivers clap their hands
  and the mountains sing joyfully
    in the LORD's presence
      because he is coming to judge the earth.
      He will judge the world with justice
        and its people with fairness.

Psalm 98:8-9

The LORD does what is right and fair
  for all who are oppressed.

He let Moses know his ways.
   He let the Israelites know the things he had done.
The LORD is compassionate, merciful, patient,
   and always ready to forgive.

Psalm 103:6-8

He is the LORD our God.
   His judgments are pronounced
      throughout the earth.
He always remembers his promise,
   the word that he commanded
      for a thousand generations.

Psalm 105:7-8

Hallelujah!

Give thanks to the LORD because he is good,
   because his mercy endures forever.
Who can speak about all the mighty things
      the LORD has done?
Who can announce all the things for which
      he is worthy of praise?
Blessed are those who defend justice
   and do what is right at all times.

Psalm 106:1-3

The LORD will provide justice for his people
   and have compassion on his servants.

Psalm 135:14

The LORD remains faithful forever.
   He brings about justice for those who are oppressed.
   He gives food to those who are hungry.
The LORD sets prisoners free.

The LORD gives sight to blind people.
The LORD straightens the backs of those
    who are bent over.
The LORD loves righteous people.

Psalm 146:6-8

The LORD will be our mighty defender
    in a place surrounded by wide rivers and streams.
        Ships with oars won't travel on them.
        Stately ships won't sail on them.
The LORD is our judge.
The LORD is our lawgiver.
The LORD is our king.
The LORD is our savior.

Isaiah 33:21-22

But let justice flow like a river
    and righteousness like an ever-flowing stream.

Amos 5:24

You mortals, the LORD has told you what is good.
    This is what the LORD requires from you:
        to do what is right,
            to love mercy,
                and to live humbly with your God.

Micah 6:8

Then the LORD spoke his word to Zechariah. He said, "This is what the LORD of Armies says: Administer real justice, and be compassionate and kind to each other. Don't oppress widows, orphans, foreigners, and poor people. And don't even think of doing evil to each other."

Zechariah 7:8-10

The Father doesn't judge anyone. He has entrusted judgment entirely to the Son so that everyone will honor the Son as they honor the Father. Whoever doesn't honor the Son doesn't honor the Father who sent him. I can guarantee this truth: Those who listen to what I say and believe in the one who sent me will have eternal life. They won't be judged because they have already passed from death to life.

John 5:22-24

Love and Compassion

Your kindness is so great!
  You reserve it for those who fear you.
    Adam's descendants watch
      as you show it to those who take refuge in you.
  You hide them in the secret place of your presence
    from those who scheme against them.
  You keep them in a shelter,
    safe from quarrelsome tongues.

                                        Psalm 31:19-20

As high as the heavens are above the earth—
  that is how vast his mercy is toward those
    who fear him.
As far as the east is from the west—
  that is how far he has removed our rebellious acts
    from himself.

                                        Psalm 103:11-12

As a father has compassion for his children,
  so the LORD has compassion for those
    who fear him.

He certainly knows what we are made of.
  He bears in mind that we are dust.
Human life is as short-lived as grass.
  It blossoms like a flower in the field.

When the wind blows over the flower,
    it disappears,
       and there is no longer any sign of it.

Psalm 103:13-16

Can a woman forget her nursing child?
Will she have no compassion on the child from her
    womb?
Although mothers may forget,
    I will not forget you.
I have engraved you on the palms of my hands.
    Your walls are always in my presence.

Isaiah 49:15-16

The LORD appeared to me in a faraway place and said,

"I love you with an everlasting love.
    So I will continue to show you my kindness."

Jeremiah 31:3

Jesus went to all the towns and villages. He taught in the synagogues and spread the Good News of the kingdom. He also cured every disease and sickness. When he saw the crowds, he felt sorry for them. They were troubled and helpless like sheep without a shepherd. Then he said to his disciples, "The harvest is large, but the workers are few. So ask the Lord who gives this harvest to send workers to harvest his crops."

Matthew 9:35-38

Some people brought infants to Jesus to have him hold them. When the disciples saw this, they told the people not to do that. But Jesus called the infants to him and said, "Don't stop the children from coming to me! Children like these are part of the kingdom of God. I can guarantee this truth: Whoever doesn't receive the kingdom of God as a little child receives it will never enter it."

Luke 18:15-17

Father, I want those you have given to me to be with me, to be where I am. I want them to see my glory, which you gave me because you loved me before the world was made. Righteous Father, the world didn't know you. Yet, I knew you, and these disciples have known that you sent me. I have made your name known to them, and I will make it known so that the love you have for me will be in them and I will be in them.

John 17:24-26

What will separate us from the love Christ has for us? Can trouble, distress, persecution, hunger, nakedness, danger, or violent death separate us from his love?

Romans 8:35

Clearly, Christ's love guides us. We are convinced of the fact that one man has died for all people. Therefore, all people have died. He died for all people so that those who live should no longer live for themselves but for the man who died and was brought back to life for them.

2 Corinthians 5:14-15

The Lord Almighty says, "I will be your Father, and you will be my sons and daughters."

2 Corinthians 6:18

This way, with all of God's people you will be able to understand how wide, long, high, and deep his love is. You will know Christ's love, which goes far beyond any knowledge. I am praying this so that you may be completely filled with God.

God our Father loved us and by his kindness gave us everlasting encouragement and good hope. Together with our Lord Jesus Christ, may he encourage and strengthen you to do and say everything that is good.

2 Thessalonians 2:16-17

My child, find your source of strength in the kindness of Christ Jesus.

2 Timothy 2:1

This is love: not that we have loved God, but that he loved us and sent his Son to be the payment for our sins. Dear friends, if this is the way God loved us, we must also love each other.

1 John 4:10-11

God's love has reached its goal in us. So we look ahead with confidence to the day of judgment. While we are in this world, we are exactly like him with regard to love.

1 John 4:17

Mercy

But I trust your mercy.
My heart finds joy in your salvation.
I will sing to the LORD because he has been good to me.

Psalm 13:5-6

I see your mercy in front of me.
I walk in the light of your truth.

Psalm 26:3

I will rejoice and be glad because of your mercy.
You have seen my misery.
You have known the troubles in my soul.
You have not handed me over to the enemy.
You have set my feet in a place
where I can move freely.

Psalm 31:7-8

O LORD, your mercy reaches to the heavens,
your faithfulness to the skies.
Your righteousness is like the mountains of God,
your judgments like the deep ocean.
You save people and animals, O LORD.

Psalm 36:5-6

Your mercy is so precious, O God,
that Adam's descendants take refuge
in the shadow of your wings.

They are refreshed with the rich foods in your house,
   and you make them drink
      from the river of your pleasure.

Psalm 36:7-8

Sing a new song to the LORD
   because he has done miraculous things.
      His right hand and his holy arm
         have gained victory for him.
The LORD has made his salvation known.
   He has uncovered his righteousness for the nations
      to see.
   He has not forgotten to be merciful and faithful.

Psalm 98:1-3

He has made his miracles unforgettable.
   The LORD is merciful and compassionate.
He provides food for those who fear him.
He always remembers his promise.

Psalm 111:4-5

Let your mercy comfort me
   as you promised.
Let your compassion reach me so that I may live,
   because your teachings make me happy.

Psalm 119:76-77

Have pity on us, O LORD.
Have pity on us
   because we have suffered more than our share
      of contempt.
We have suffered more than our share of ridicule
   from those who are carefree.
We have suffered more than our share of contempt
   from those who are arrogant.

Psalm 123:3-4

Let me hear about your mercy in the morning,
  because I trust you.
Let me know the way that I should go,
  because I long for you.

Psalm 143:8

The Lord is good to everyone
  and has compassion for everything
    that he has made.
Everything that you have made will give thanks to you,
  O Lord,
  and your faithful ones will praise you.
Everyone will talk about the glory of your kingdom
  and will tell the descendants of Adam
    about your might
    in order to make known your mighty deeds
      and the glorious honor of your kingdom.
Your kingdom is an everlasting kingdom.
Your empire endures throughout every generation.

Psalm 145:9-13

Blessed are those who hunger and thirst for God's
  approval.
  They will be satisfied.
Blessed are those who show mercy.
  They will be treated mercifully.

Matthew 5:6-7

What can we say—that God is unfair? That's unthinkable!
For example, God said to Moses, "I will be kind to anyone I
want to. I will be merciful to anyone I want to." Therefore,
God's choice does not depend on a person's desire or effort,
but on God's mercy.

Romans 9:14-16

Peace

The LORD will give power to his people.
The LORD will bless his people with peace.

Psalm 29:11

With his peace, he will rescue my soul
   from the war waged against me,
      because there are many soldiers
         fighting against me.
God will listen.
   The one who has sat enthroned from the beginning
     will deal with them.

Psalm 55:18-19

I want to hear what God the LORD says,
   because he promises peace to his people,
     to his godly ones.
     But they must not go back to their stupidity.
Indeed, his salvation is near those who fear him,
   and his glory will remain in our land.

Psalm 85:8-9

A tranquil heart makes for a healthy body,
   but jealousy is like bone cancer.

Proverbs 14:30

With perfect peace you will protect
   those whose minds cannot be changed,
   because they trust you.

Isaiah 26:3

This is what the LORD says:

I will offer you peace like a river
   and the wealth of the nations like an overflowing
      stream.
      You will nurse and be carried in Jerusalem's arms
         and cuddled on her knees.
As a mother comforts her child,
   so will I comfort you.
      You will be comforted in Jerusalem.
When you see it, your heart will rejoice
   and you will flourish like new grass.
The power of the LORD will be made known to his
      servants,
   but he will condemn his enemies.

Isaiah 66:12-14

I will promise them peace. I will remove the wild animals
from the land so that my sheep can live safely in the wilderness and sleep in the woods.

Ezekiel 34:25

Blessed are those who make peace.
   They will be called God's children.

Matthew 5:9

I'm leaving you peace. I'm giving you my peace. I don't
give you the kind of peace that the world gives. So don't
be troubled or cowardly.

John 14:27

I've told you this so that my peace will be with you. In the world you'll have trouble. But cheer up! I have overcome the world.

John 16:33

He is our peace. In his body he has made Jewish and non-Jewish people one by breaking down the wall of hostility that kept them apart. He brought an end to the commandments and demands found in Moses' Teachings so that he could take Jewish and non-Jewish people and create one new humanity in himself. So he made peace.

Ephesians 2:14-15

The wisdom that comes from above is first of all pure. Then it is peaceful, gentle, obedient, filled with mercy and good deeds, impartial, and sincere. A harvest that has God's approval comes from the peace planted by peacemakers.

James 3:17-18

Perseverance

But I call on God,
  and the LORD saves me.
Morning, noon, and night I complain and groan,
  and he listens to my voice.

Psalm 55:16-17

You have made me endure many terrible troubles.
You restore me to life again.
You bring me back from the depths of the earth.

Psalm 71:20

It's not that I've already reached the goal or have already
completed the course. But I run to win that which Jesus
Christ has already won for me. Brothers and sisters, I can't
consider myself a winner yet. This is what I do: I don't
look back, I lengthen my stride, and I run straight toward
the goal to win the prize that God's heavenly call offers
in Christ Jesus.

Philippians 3:12-14

Concentrate on reading Scripture in worship, giving encouraging messages, and teaching people. . . . Practice these
things. Devote your life to them so that everyone can see
your progress. Focus on your life and your teaching. Continue to do what I've told you. If you do this, you will save
yourself and those who hear you.

1 Timothy 4:13-16

Since we are surrounded by so many examples of faith, we must get rid of everything that slows us down, especially sin that distracts us. We must run the race that lies ahead of us and never give up. We must focus on Jesus, the source and goal of our faith. He saw the joy ahead of him, so he endured death on the cross and ignored the disgrace it brought him. Then he received the highest position in heaven, the one next to the throne of God. Think about Jesus, who endured opposition from sinners, so that you don't become tired and give up.

Hebrews 12:1-3

Strengthen your tired arms and weak knees. Keep walking along straight paths so that your injured leg won't get worse. Instead, let it heal.

Hebrews 12:12-13

Blessed are those who endure when they are tested. When they pass the test, they will receive the crown of life that God has promised to those who love him.

James 1:12

Prayer

I call aloud to the LORD,
    and he answers me from his holy mountain. *Selah*
I lie down and sleep.
I wake up again because the LORD continues
      to support me.
I am not afraid of the tens of thousands
    who have taken positions against me on all sides.

Psalm 3:4-6

Know that the LORD singles out godly people
    for himself.
    The LORD hears me when I call to him.

Psalm 4:3

I call to God Most High,
    to the God who does everything for me.
He sends his help from heaven and saves me.
He disgraces the one who is harassing me. *Selah*
God sends his mercy and his truth!

Psalm 57:2-3

But God has heard me.
    He has paid attention to my prayer.

Thanks be to God,
    who has not rejected my prayer
      or taken away his mercy from me.

Psalm 66:19-20

May my prayer come to you at an acceptable time,
O Lord.
O God, out of the greatness of your mercy,
answer me with the truth of your salvation.
Rescue me from the mud.
Do not let me sink into it.

Psalm 69:13-14

I have become an example to many people,
but you are my strong refuge.
My mouth is filled with your praise,
with your glory all day long.

Psalm 71:7-8

He will turn his attention to the prayers
of those who have been abandoned.
He will not despise their prayers.

Psalm 102:17

The Lord looked down from his holy place
high above.
From heaven he looked at the earth.
He heard the groans of the prisoners
and set free those who were
condemned to death.

Psalm 102:19-20

Give thanks to the Lord because he is good,
because his mercy endures forever.

Let the people the Lord defended repeat these words.
In their distress they cried out to the Lord.
He rescued them from their troubles.

Psalm 107:1-2, 6

During times of trouble I called on the LORD.
The LORD answered me and set me free
from all of them.
The LORD is on my side.
I am not afraid.
What can mortals do to me?
The LORD is on my side as my helper.
I will see the defeat of those who hate me.

Psalm 118:5-7

I have called out with all my heart. Answer me,
O LORD.
I want to obey your laws.
I have called out.
Save me, so that I can obey your written
instructions.
I got up before dawn, and I cried out for help.
My hope is based on your word.
My eyes are wide-open throughout the nighttime
hours
to reflect on your word.
In keeping with your mercy, hear my voice.
O LORD, give me a new life guided by your
regulations.

Psalm 119:145-149

When I was in trouble, I cried out to the LORD,
and he answered me.

Psalm 120:1

When I called, you answered me.
You made me bold by strengthening my soul.

Psalm 138:3

The LORD is near to everyone who prays to him,
    to every faithful person who prays to him.
He fills the needs of those who fear him.
He hears their cries for help and saves them.
The LORD protects everyone who loves him.

Psalm 145:18-20

O LORD, you are my God.
I will highly honor you; I will praise your name.
    You have done miraculous things.
    You have been completely reliable
        in carrying out your plans from long ago.
You have been a refuge for the poor,
    a refuge for the needy in their distress,
    a shelter from the rain, and shade from the heat.

Isaiah 25:1, 4

Before they call, I will answer.
While they're still speaking, I will hear.

Isaiah 65:24

The LORD is far from wicked people,
    but he hears the prayers of righteous people.

Proverbs 15:29

You will call to me. You will come and pray to me, and
I will hear you. When you look for me, you will find me.
When you wholeheartedly seek me, I will let you find me,
declares the LORD.

Jeremiah 29:12-14

Jesus replied to them, "My Father is working right now,
and so am I."

John 5:17

I pray for them. I'm not praying for the world but for those you gave me, because they are yours.

John 17:9

For this reason we have not stopped praying for you since the day we heard about you. We ask God to fill you with the knowledge of his will through every kind of spiritual wisdom and insight. We ask this so that you will live the kind of lives that prove you belong to the Lord. Then you will want to please him in every way as you grow in producing every kind of good work by this knowledge about God.

Colossians 1:9-10

I constantly remember you in my prayers night and day when I thank God, whom I serve with a clear conscience as my ancestors did. I remember your tears and want to see you so that I can be filled with happiness. I'm reminded of how sincere your faith is.

2 Timothy 1:3-5

If any of you are having trouble, pray. If you are happy, sing psalms.

James 5:13

We are confident that God listens to us if we ask for anything that has his approval. We know that he listens to our requests. So we know that we already have what we ask him for.

1 John 5:13-14

If you are sick, call for the church leaders. Have them pray for you and anoint you with olive oil in the name of the Lord. (Prayers offered in faith will save those who are sick, and the Lord will cure them.) If you have sinned, you will be forgiven.

James 5:14-15

Salvation

My soul will find joy in the LORD
and be joyful about his salvation.

Psalm 35:9

Remember me, O LORD, when you show favor
to your people.
Come to help me with your salvation.

Psalm 106:4

He has sent salvation to his people.
He has ordered that his promise
should continue forever.

Psalm 111:9

The people ransomed by the LORD will return.
They will come to Zion singing with joy.
Everlasting happiness will be on their heads
as a crown.
They will be glad and joyful.
They will have no sorrow or grief.

Isaiah 35:10

Turn to me and be saved, all who live at the ends of
the earth,
because I am God, and there is no other.

Isaiah 45:22

This is what the LORD says:

> In the time of favor I will answer you.
> In the day of salvation I will help you.
> I will protect you.
> I will appoint you as my promise to the people.
>> You will restore the land.
>> You will make them inherit the desolate inheritance.

Isaiah 49:8

> The LORD is not too weak to save
>> or his ear too deaf to hear.

Isaiah 59:1

What do you think? Suppose a man has 100 sheep and one of them strays. Won't he leave the 99 sheep in the hills to look for the one that has strayed? I can guarantee this truth: If he finds it, he is happier about it than about the 99 that have not strayed. In the same way, your Father in heaven does not want one of these little ones to be lost.

Matthew 18:12-14

Indeed, the Son of Man has come to seek and to save people who are lost.

Luke 19:10

However, he gave the right to become God's children to everyone who believed in him.

John 1:12

Everyone whom the Father gives me will come to me. I will never turn away anyone who comes to me. I haven't come from heaven to do what I want to do. I've come to do what the one who sent me wants me to do. The one who sent me doesn't want me to lose any of those he gave me. He wants me to bring them back to life on the last day. My Father wants all those who see the Son and believe in him to have eternal life. He wants me to bring them back to life on the last day.

John 6:37-40

I am the good shepherd. The good shepherd gives his life for the sheep. A hired hand isn't a shepherd and doesn't own the sheep. When he sees a wolf coming, he abandons the sheep and quickly runs away. So the wolf drags the sheep away and scatters the flock. The hired hand is concerned about what he's going to get paid and not about the sheep. I am the good shepherd. I know my sheep as the Father knows me. My sheep know me as I know the Father. So I give my life for my sheep.

John 10:11-15

"This world is being judged now. The ruler of this world will be thrown out now. When I have been lifted up from the earth, I will draw all people toward me." By saying this, he indicated how he was going to die.

John 12:31-32

Christ died for us while we were still sinners. This demonstrates God's love for us.

Romans 5:8

Now you have been freed from sin and have become God's slaves. This results in a holy life and, finally, in everlasting life. The payment for sin is death, but the gift that God freely gives is everlasting life found in Christ Jesus our Lord.

Romans 6:22-23

What can we say about all of this? If God is for us, who can be against us? God didn't spare his own Son but handed him over to death for all of us. So he will also give us everything along with him.

Romans 8:31-32

If you declare that Jesus is Lord, and believe that God brought him back to life, you will be saved. By believing you receive God's approval, and by declaring your faith you are saved.

Romans 10:9-10

Sin gives death its sting, and God's standards give sin its power. Thank God that he gives us the victory through our Lord Jesus Christ.

1 Corinthians 15:56-57

Good will and peace from God the Father and our Lord Jesus Christ are yours! In order to free us from this present evil world, Christ took the punishment for our sins, because that was what our God and Father wanted.

Galatians 1:3-4

I no longer live, but Christ lives in me. The life I now live I live by believing in God's Son, who loved me and took the punishment for my sins.

Galatians 2:20

You are all God's children by believing in Christ Jesus. Clearly, all of you who were baptized in Christ's name have clothed yourselves with Christ.

Galatians 3:26-27

Because you are God's children, God has sent the Spirit of his Son into us to call out, "Abba! Father!" So you are no longer slaves but God's children. Since you are God's children, God has also made you heirs.

Galatians 4:6-7

Before the creation of the world, he chose us through Christ to be holy and perfect in his presence.

Ephesians 1:4

Because of his love he had already decided to adopt us through Jesus Christ. He freely chose to do this so that the kindness he had given us in his dear Son would be praised and given glory. Through the blood of his Son, we are set free from our sins. God forgives our failures because of his overflowing kindness. He poured out his kindness by giving us every kind of wisdom and insight when he revealed the mystery of his plan to us. He had decided to do this through Christ.

Ephesians 1:5-9

God's favor has been given to each of us. It was measured out to us by Christ who gave it. That's why the Scriptures say: "When he went to the highest place, he took captive those who had captured us and gave gifts to people."

Ephesians 4:7-8

We, however, are citizens of heaven. We look forward to the Lord Jesus Christ coming from heaven as our Savior. Through his power to bring everything under his authority, he will change our humble bodies and make them like his glorified body.

Philippians 3:20-21

God has rescued us from the power of darkness and has brought us into the kingdom of his Son, whom he loves. His Son paid the price to free us, which means that our sins are forgiven.

Colossians 1:13-14

Therefore, let no one judge you because of what you eat or drink or about the observance of annual holy days, New Moon Festivals, or weekly worship days. These are a shadow of the things to come, but the body that casts the shadow belongs to Christ.

Colossians 2:16-17

This is a statement that can be trusted:

If we have died with him, we will live with him.
If we endure, we will rule with him.
If we disown him, he will disown us.
If we are unfaithful, he remains faithful
    because he cannot be untrue to himself.

2 Timothy 2:11-13

Praise the God and Father of our Lord Jesus Christ! God has given us a new birth because of his great mercy. We have been born into a new life that has a confidence which is alive because Jesus Christ has come back to life. We have been born into a new life which has an inheritance that can't be destroyed or corrupted and can't fade away. That inheritance is kept in heaven for you, since you are guarded by God's power through faith for a salvation that is ready to be revealed at the end of time.

1 Peter 1:3-5

You are coming to Christ, the living stone who was rejected by humans but was chosen as precious by God. You come to him as living stones, a spiritual house that is being built into a holy priesthood.

1 Peter 2:4-5

This is the testimony: God has given us eternal life, and this life is found in his Son. The person who has the Son has this life. The person who doesn't have the Son of God doesn't have this life.

1 John 5:11-12

Security

God is not like people. He tells no lies.
  He is not like humans. He doesn't change his mind.
    When he says something, he does it.
    When he makes a promise, he keeps it.

Numbers 23:19

The LORD rewarded me
  because of my righteousness,
  because my hands are clean.
He paid me back
  because I have kept the ways of the LORD
    and I have not wickedly turned away from
      my God,
  because all his judgments are in front of me
    and I have not turned away from his laws.
    I was innocent as far as he was concerned.
    I have kept myself from guilt.

2 Samuel 22:21-24

You bless righteous people, O LORD.
Like a large shield, you surround them
  with your favor.

Psalm 5:12

The promises of the LORD are pure,
   like silver refined in a furnace
      and purified seven times.

                Psalm 12:6

The LORD is my shepherd.
   I am never in need.
      He makes me lie down in green pastures.
      He leads me beside peaceful waters.

                Psalm 23:1-2

You are my hiding place.
You protect me from trouble.
You surround me with joyous songs of salvation.

                Selah

                Psalm 32:7

Blessed is the nation whose God is the LORD.
Blessed are the people he has chosen as his own.

                Psalm 33:12

A person's steps are directed by the LORD,
   and the LORD delights in his way.
When he falls, he will not be thrown down headfirst
   because the LORD holds on to his hand.

                Psalm 37:23-24

Righteous people will inherit the land
   and live there permanently.

                Psalm 37:29

Wait with hope for the LORD, and follow his path,
   and he will honor you by giving you the land.
      When wicked people are cut off, you will see it.

                Psalm 37:34

The victory for righteous people comes
        from the LORD.
    He is their fortress in times of trouble.
The LORD helps them and rescues them.
He rescues them from wicked people.
He saves them because they have taken refuge in him.

Psalm 37:39-40

Righteous people will rejoice
        when they see God take revenge.
They will wash their feet
        in the blood of wicked people.
Then people will say,
    "Righteous people certainly have a reward.
    There is a God who judges on earth."

Psalm 58:10-11

Blessed is the person you choose
        and invite to live with you in your courtyards.
            We will be filled with good food from your house,
                from your holy temple.

Psalm 65:4

You answer us with awe-inspiring acts
        done in righteousness,
    O God, our savior,
        the hope of all the ends of the earth
            and of the most distant sea,
        the one who set the mountains in place
            with his strength,
        the one who is clothed with power,
        the one who calms the roar of the seas,
            their crashing waves,
                and the uproar of the nations.

Those who live at the ends of the earth are in awe
    of your miraculous signs.
The lands of the morning sunrise and evening sunset
    sing joyfully.

Psalm 65:5-8

Our God is the God of victories.
The Almighty Lord is our escape from death.

Psalm 68:20

Your God has decided you will be strong.
    Display your strength, O God,
        as you have for us before.

Psalm 68:28

My heart is confident, O God.
I want to sing and make music even with my soul.
    Wake up, harp and lyre!
I want to wake up at dawn.
I want to give thanks to you among the people,
    O Lord.
I want to make music to praise you among the nations
    because your mercy is higher than the heavens.
        Your truth reaches the skies.

Psalm 108:1-4

Hallelujah!

Blessed is the person who fears the Lord
    and is happy to obey his commands.
        He is not afraid of bad news.
        His heart remains secure, full of confidence
            in the Lord.
        His heart is steady, and he is not afraid.

In the end he will look triumphantly
at his enemies.

Psalm 112:1, 7-8

All goes well for the person who is generous
and lends willingly.
He earns an honest living.
He will never fail.
A righteous person will always be remembered.

Psalm 112:5-6

I was glad when they said to me,
"Let's go to the house of the LORD."
For the sake of the house of the LORD our God,
I will seek what is good for you.

Psalm 122:1, 9

The LORD is righteous.
He has cut me loose
from the ropes that wicked people tied
around me.

Psalm 129:4

How precious are your thoughts concerning me,
O God!
How vast in number they are!
If I try to count them,
there would be more of them
than there are grains of sand.
When I wake up, I am still with you.

Psalm 139:17-18

Thank the LORD, my rock,
  who trained my hands to fight
    and my fingers to do battle,
  my merciful one, my fortress,
  my stronghold, and my savior,
  my shield, the one in whom I take refuge,
    and the one who brings people
      under my authority.

Psalm 144:1-2

Blessings cover the head of a righteous person,
  but violence covers the mouths of wicked people.

The name of a righteous person remains blessed,
  but the names of wicked people will rot away.

Proverbs 10:6-7

The righteousness of innocent people
  makes their road smooth,
  but wicked people fall by their own wickedness.

Proverbs 11:5

A good person obtains favor from the LORD,
  but the LORD condemns everyone who schemes.

Proverbs 12:2

An evil person is trapped by his own sinful talk,
  but a righteous person escapes from trouble.

Proverbs 12:13

Righteousness protects the honest way of life,
  but wickedness ruins a sacrifice for sin.

Proverbs 13:6

Entrust your efforts to the LORD,
   and your plans will succeed.

> Proverbs 16:3

My people will live in a peaceful place,
   in safe homes and quiet places of rest.

> Isaiah 32:18

I can guarantee that the Son of Man will acknowledge in front of God's angels every person who acknowledges him in front of others.

> Luke 12:8

My sheep respond to my voice, and I know who they are. They follow me, and I give them eternal life. They will never be lost, and no one will tear them away from me. My Father, who gave them to me, is greater than everyone else, and no one can tear them away from my Father.

> John 10:27-29

I don't call you servants anymore, because a servant doesn't know what his master is doing. But I've called you friends because I've made known to you everything that I've heard from my Father. You didn't choose me, but I chose you. I have appointed you to go, to produce fruit that will last, and to ask the Father in my name to give you whatever you ask for.

> John 15:15-16

Now, dear children, live in Christ. Then, when he appears we will have confidence, and when he comes we won't turn from him in shame. If you know that Christ has God's approval, you also know that everyone who does what God approves of has been born from God.

> 1 John 2:28-29

Sexual Integrity

O Lord, who may stay in your tent?
Who may live on your holy mountain?

The one who walks with integrity,
    does what is righteous,
    and speaks the truth within his heart.

The one who does not slander with his tongue,
    do evil to a friend,
    or bring disgrace on his neighbor.

Psalm 15:1-3

How can a young person keep his life pure?
    He can do it by holding on to your word.
I find joy in the way shown by your written
        instructions
    more than I find joy in all kinds of riches.

Psalm 119:9, 14

Young women of Jerusalem, swear to me
    by the gazelles
        or by the does in the field,
            that you will not awaken love
                or arouse love before its proper time.

Song of Solomon 3:5

Blessed are those whose thoughts are pure.
They will see God.

Matthew 5:8

Each of you should know that finding a husband or wife for yourself is to be done in a holy and honorable way, not in the passionate, lustful way of people who don't know God. No one should take advantage of or exploit other believers that way. The Lord is the one who punishes people for all these things. We've already told you and warned you about this. God didn't call us to be sexually immoral but to be holy.

1 Thessalonians 4:4-7

Because of this, make every effort to add integrity to your faith; and to integrity add knowledge; to knowledge add self-control; to self-control add endurance; to endurance add godliness; to godliness add Christian affection; and to Christian affection add love. If you have these qualities and they are increasing, it demonstrates that your knowledge about our Lord Jesus Christ is living and productive.

2 Peter 1:5-9

Significance

The LORD will bless you and watch over you.
   The LORD will smile on you and be kind to you.
      The LORD will look on you with favor and give
         you peace.

                          Numbers 6:24-26

The LORD, who is always thinking about us,
   will bless us.
   He will bless those who fear the LORD,
      from the least important to the most important.
May the LORD continue to bless you
   and your children.
You will be blessed by the LORD,
   the maker of heaven and earth.

                          Psalm 115:12-15

Blessed are those whose lives have integrity,
   those who follow the teachings of the LORD.

                          Psalm 119:1

O LORD, you have examined me, and you know me.
   You alone know when I sit down and when I get up.
   You read my thoughts from far away.
   You watch me when I travel and when I rest.
   You are familiar with all my ways.
      Even before there is a single word on my tongue,

> you know all about it, LORD.
> You are all around me—in front of me
>   and in back of me.
> You lay your hand on me.
>   Such knowledge is beyond my grasp.
>   It is so high I cannot reach it.

Psalm 139:1-6

> Charm is deceptive, and beauty evaporates,
>   but a woman who has the fear of the LORD
>   should be praised.

Proverbs 31:30

This is what the LORD, your Defender, the Holy One of Israel, says:

> I am the LORD your God.
>   I teach you what is best for you.
>   I lead you where you should go.

Isaiah 48:17

> But now, LORD, you are our Father.
>   We are the clay, and you are our potter.
>   We are the work of your hands.

Isaiah 64:8

> After this, I will pour my Spirit on everyone.
>   Your sons and daughters will prophesy.
>   Your old men will dream dreams.
>   Your young men will see visions.
> In those days I will pour my Spirit on servants,
>   on both men and women.

Joel 2:28-29

You are already clean because of what I have told you. Live in me, and I will live in you. A branch cannot produce any fruit by itself. It has to stay attached to the vine. In the same way, you cannot produce fruit unless you live in me. I am the vine. You are the branches. Those who live in me while I live in them will produce a lot of fruit. But you can't produce anything without me.

John 15:3-5

If you live in me and what I say lives in you, then ask for anything you want, and it will be yours. You give glory to my Father when you produce a lot of fruit and therefore show that you are my disciples.

John 15:7-8

Peter said, "Now I understand that God doesn't play favorites. Rather, whoever respects God and does what is right is acceptable to him in any nation."

Acts 10:35-36

God in his kindness gave each of us different gifts. If your gift is speaking God's word, make sure what you say agrees with the Christian faith. If your gift is serving, then devote yourself to serving. If it is teaching, devote yourself to teaching. If it is encouraging others, devote yourself to giving encouragement. If it is sharing, be generous. If it is leadership, lead enthusiastically. If it is helping people in need, help them cheerfully.

Romans 12:6-8

But as Scripture says:

"No eye has seen,
    no ear has heard,
        and no mind has imagined

163

the things that God has prepared
for those who love him."

1 Corinthians 2:9

God has revealed those things to us by his Spirit. The Spirit searches everything, especially the deep things of God. After all, who knows everything about a person except that person's own spirit? In the same way, no one has known everything about God except God's Spirit. Now, we didn't receive the spirit that belongs to the world. Instead, we received the Spirit who comes from God so that we could know the things which God has freely given us.

1 Corinthians 2:10-12

There are different spiritual gifts, but the same Spirit gives them. There are different ways of serving, and yet the same Lord is served. There are different types of work to do, but the same God produces every gift in every person.

1 Corinthians 12:4-6

Our bodies are made of clay, yet we have the treasure of the Good News in them. This shows that the superior power of this treasure belongs to God and doesn't come from us.

2 Corinthians 4:7

I pray that the glorious Father, the God of our Lord Jesus Christ, would give you a spirit of wisdom and revelation as you come to know Christ better. Then you will have deeper insight. You will know the confidence that he calls you to have and the glorious wealth that God's people will inherit. You will also know the unlimited greatness of his power as it works with might and strength for us, the believers. He worked with that same power in Christ when he brought him back to life and gave him the highest position in heaven.

Ephesians 1:17-20

May the God who gives peace make you holy in every way. May he keep your whole being—spirit, soul, and body—blameless when our Lord Jesus Christ comes. The one who calls you is faithful, and he will do this.

1 Thessalonians 5:23-24

God's divine power has given us everything we need for life and for godliness. This power was given to us through knowledge of the one who called us by his own glory and integrity. Through his glory and integrity he has given us his promises that are of the highest value. Through these promises you will share in the divine nature because you have escaped the corruption that sinful desires cause in the world.

2 Peter 1:3-4

The one who is testifying to these things says, "Yes, I'm coming soon!" Amen! Come, Lord Jesus! The good will of the Lord Jesus be with all of you. Amen!

Revelation 22:20-21

Support/Strength

He will send you help from his holy place
  and support you from Zion.
He will remember all your grain offerings
  and look with favor on your burnt offerings.   *Selah*
                                              Psalm 20:1-3

God, the God of Israel, is awe-inspiring
    in his holy place.
  He gives strength and power to his people.
    Thanks be to God!

                                              Psalm 68:35

O God, your ways are holy!
    What god is as great as our God?
You are the God who performs miracles.
You have made your strength known
    among the nations.
                                              Psalm 77:13-14

Blessed are those who find strength in you.
    Their hearts are on the road that leads to you.
      As they pass through a valley
        where balsam trees grow,
      they make it a place of springs.
        The early rains cover it with blessings.

Their strength grows as they go along
until each one of them appears
in front of God in Zion.

Psalm 84:5-7

The LORD will answer you in times of trouble.
The name of the God of Jacob will protect you.
If the LORD does not build the house,
  it is useless for the builders to work on it.
If the LORD does not protect a city,
  it is useless for the guard to stay alert.
It is useless to work hard for the food you eat
  by getting up early and going to bed late.
   The LORD gives food to those he loves
    while they sleep.

Psalm 127:1-2

Holy Father, keep them safe by the power of your name, the name that you gave me, so that their unity may be like ours.

John 17:11

At the same time the Spirit also helps us in our weakness, because we don't know how to pray for what we need. But the Spirit intercedes along with our groans that cannot be expressed in words. The one who searches our hearts knows what the Spirit has in mind. The Spirit intercedes for God's people the way God wants him to.

Romans 8:26-27

He makes the whole body fit together and unites it through the support of every joint. As each and every part does its job, he makes the body grow so that it builds itself up in love.

Ephesians 4:16

We ask him to strengthen you by his glorious might with all the power you need to patiently endure everything with joy. You will also thank the Father, who has made you able to share the light, which is what God's people inherit.

Colossians 1:11-12

God, who shows you his kindness and who has called you through Christ Jesus to his eternal glory, will restore you, strengthen you, make you strong, and support you as you suffer for a little while.

1 Peter 5:10

Truth

The teachings of the LORD are perfect.
   They renew the soul.
The testimony of the LORD is dependable.
   It makes gullible people wise.
The instructions of the LORD are correct.
   They make the heart rejoice.
The command of the LORD is radiant.
   It makes the eyes shine.

Psalm 19:7-8

Send your light and your truth.
   Let them guide me.
   Let them bring me to your holy mountain
      and to your dwelling place.

Psalm 43:3

Truth sprouts from the ground,
   and righteousness looks down from heaven.
The LORD will certainly give us what is good,
   and our land will produce crops.
Righteousness will go ahead of him
   and make a path for his steps.

Psalm 85:11-13

His works are done with truth and justice.
   All his guiding principles are trustworthy.

They last forever and ever.
They are carried out with truth and decency.

Psalm 111:7-8

Even though influential people plot against me,
I reflect on your laws.
Indeed, your written instructions make me happy.
They are my best friends.

Psalm 119:23-24

I remembered your regulations from long ago,
O Lord,
and I found comfort in them.

Psalm 119:52

It was good that I had to suffer
in order to learn your laws.
The teachings that come from your mouth
are worth more to me
than thousands in gold or silver.

Psalm 119:71-72

My soul is weak from waiting for you to save me.
My hope is based on your word.
My eyes have become strained from looking
for your promise.
I ask, "When will you comfort me?"
Although I have become like a shriveled
and dried out wineskin,
I have not forgotten your laws.

Psalm 119:81-83

O Lord, your word is established in heaven forever.
Your faithfulness endures

throughout every generation.
You set the earth in place,
    and it continues to stand.
All things continue to stand today
    because of your regulations,
    since they are all your servants.
If your teachings had not made me happy,
  then I would have died in my misery.

Psalm 119:89-92

Your word is a lamp for my feet
  and a light for my path.

Psalm 119:105

Trouble and hardship have found me,
  but your commandments still make me happy.
Your written instructions are always right.
  Help me understand them so that I will live.

Psalm 119:143-144

Fasten them around your neck.
Write them on the tablet of your heart.
  Then you will find favor and much success
    in the sight of God and humanity.

Proverbs 3:3-4

The word of truth lasts forever,
  but lies last only a moment. . . .
Lips that lie are disgusting to the LORD,
  but honest people are his delight.

Proverbs 12:19, 22

Wisdom

The Lord says,
  "I will instruct you.
  I will teach you the way that you should go.
  I will advise you as my eyes watch over you."

Psalm 32:8

The fear of the Lord is the beginning of knowledge.
Stubborn fools despise wisdom and discipline.

Proverbs 1:7

My son,
  if you take my words to heart
    and treasure my commands within you,
  if you pay close attention to wisdom,
    and let your mind reach for understanding,
  if indeed you call out for insight,
  if you ask aloud for understanding,
  if you search for wisdom as if it were money
    and hunt for it as if it were hidden treasure,
  then you will understand the fear of the Lord
    and you will find the knowledge of God.
  The Lord gives wisdom.
    From his mouth come knowledge
      and understanding.

Proverbs 2:1-6

Blessed is the one who finds wisdom
and the one who obtains understanding.
The profit gained from wisdom is greater than
the profit gained from silver.
Its yield is better than fine gold.
Proverbs 3:13-14

Acquire wisdom.
Acquire understanding.
Do not forget.
Do not turn away from the words
that I have spoken.
Do not abandon wisdom,
and it will watch over you.
Love wisdom, and it will protect you.
Proverbs 4:5-6

The teachings of a wise person are a fountain of life
to turn one away from the grasp of death.
Good sense brings favor,
but the way of treacherous people is always
the same.
Proverbs 13:14-15

The LORD is the one who directs a person's steps.
How then can anyone understand his own way?
Proverbs 20:24

A strong man knows how to use his strength,
but a person with knowledge is even more powerful.
Proverbs 24:5

The Holy Bible in Clear, Natural English

"GOD'S WORD® *is an easy-to-understand Bible translation....It is a wonderful version.*"
~ REV. BILLY GRAHAM

GOD'S WORD Translation (GW) communicates the saving, life-changing Good News about Jesus in clear, natural English. Translated directly from the Hebrew, Aramaic, and Greek, GW is an exceptional Bible that consciously combines scholarly fidelity with natural English.

THE COMBINATION OF ACCURACY AND READABILITY MAKES GW IDEALLY SUITED FOR THE FOLLOWING:

- Devotional reading and in-depth study
- Preaching, teaching, and worship
- Memorization
- Discipleship

BakerBooks
a division of Baker Publishing Group

GOD'S WORD®
TRANSLATION